Swarm Intelligence Methods for Statistical Regression

T0383113

Swarm Intelligence Methods for Statistical Regression

Soumya D. Mohanty

CRC Press
Taylor & Francis Group
Boca Raton London New York

CRC Press is an imprint of the
Taylor & Francis Group, an **informa** business

CRC Press
Taylor & Francis Group
6000 Broken Sound Parkway NW, Suite 300
Boca Raton, FL 33487-2742

First issued in paperback 2020

© 2019 by Taylor & Francis Group, LLC
CRC Press is an imprint of Taylor & Francis Group, an Informa business

No claim to original U.S. Government works

ISBN-13: 978-1-138-55818-2 (hbk)
ISBN-13: 978-0-367-67037-5 (pbk)

Visit the Taylor & Francis Web site at
http://www.taylorandfrancis.com

and the CRC Press Web site at
http://www.crcpress.com

Dedication
To my parents, Rama Ranjan and Krishna

Contents

Preface

This book is based on a set of lectures on big data analysis delivered at the BigDat International Winter School held at Bari, Italy, in 2017. The lectures focused on a very practical issue encountered in the statistical regression of non-linear models, namely, the numerical optimization of the fitting function. The optimization problem in statistical analysis, especially in big data applications, is often a bottleneck that forces either the adoption of simpler models or a shift to linear models even where non-linearity is known to be a better option. The goal of the lectures was to introduce the audience to a set of relatively recent biology inspired stochastic optimization methods, collectively called swarm intelligence (SI) methods, that are proving quite effective in tackling the optimization challenge in statistical analysis.

It was clear from the audience response at these lectures that, despite their collective background in very diverse areas of data analysis ranging from the natural sciences to the social media industry, many had not heard of and none had seriously explored SI methods. The root causes behind this lacuna seem to be (a) a lack of familiarity, within the data analysis community, of the latest literature in stochastic optimization, and (b) lack of experience and guidance in tuning these methods to work well in real-world problems. Matters are not helped by the fact that there are not a whole lot of papers in the optimization community examining the role of SI methods in statistical analysis, most of the focus in that field being on optimization problems in engineering.

I hope this small book helps in bridging the current divide between the two communities. As I have seen within my own research, the statistical data analyst will find that success in solving the optimization challenge spurs the contemplation of better, more sophisticated models for data. Students and researchers in the SI community reading this book will find that statistical data analysis offers a rich source of challenging test beds for their methods.

The aim of the book is to arm the reader with practical tips and rules of thumb that are observed to work well, not to provide a deeper than necessary theoretical background. In particular, the book does not delve deep into the huge range of SI methods out there, concentrating rather on one particular method, namely particle swarm optimization (PSO). My experience in teaching SI methods to students has shown that it is best to learn these methods by starting with one and understanding it well. For this purpose, PSO provides the simplest entry point. Similarly, this book does not provide a more than superficial background in optimization theory, choosing to only highlight some its important results.

It is assumed that the reader of this book has a basic background in probability theory and function approximation at the level of undergraduate or graduate courses. Nonetheless, appendices are provided that cover the required material succinctly. Instead of a problem set, two realistic statistical regression problems covering both parametric and nonparametric approaches form the workhorse exercises in this book. The reader is highly encouraged to independently implement these examples and reproduce the associated results provided in the book.

References are primarily provided in the "Notes" section at the end of each chapter. While it was tempting to include in the book a more complete review of the technical literature than what is currently provided, I decided to point the reader to mostly textbooks or review articles. This was done keeping in mind the expected readership of this book, which I assume would be similar to the student-heavy makeup of the BigDat participants. This inevitably means that many key references have been left out but I hope that the ones included will give readers a good start in seeking out the technical material that is appropriate for their application areas.

Acknowledgements: It is a pleasure to acknowledge colleagues who supported the inception and development of this book. I thank Carlos Martin-Vide, Donato Malerba, and other organizers of the BigDat schools for inviting me as a lecturer and for their hospitality. This annual school provides a wonderful and refreshing opportunity to interact with data scientists and students from a broad spectrum of fields, and I hope that it continues to have several future editions.

Before embarking on the writing of this book, I had the pleasure of discussing the core content of the lectures with Innocenzo Pinto and Luigi Troiano at the University of Sannio at Benevento, Italy. I had similar opportunities, thanks to Runqiu Liu and Zong-kuan Guo at the Chinese Academy of Sciences, Beijing, to present the material to undergraduate and graduate students during my lectures there on gravitational wave data analysis. I am greatly indebted to Yan Wang at Huazhong University of Science and Technology, Wuhan, for a thorough reading of the draft and many invaluable comments and suggestions. Several useful comments from Ram Valluri at the University of Western Ontario are appreciated as well. Finally, I thank Randi Cohen at CRC press for contacting me and initiating this project.

Conventions and Notation

Technical terms are italicized when they are introduced but appear thereafter in normal font. Italics are also used for emphasis where needed.

Much of the notation used in this book is collected here for a quick reference.

$\forall$	For all.
$A \propto B$	A is proportional to B.
$\sum_{k=i}^{j}$	Summation of quantities indexed by integer k.
$\prod_{k=i}^{j}$	Product of quantities indexed by integer k.
$\mathbb{B}$	A set. Small sets will be shown explicitly, when needed, as $\{a, b, \ldots\}$. Otherwise, $\{a \mid C\}$ will denote the set of elements for which the statement C is true. A set of indexed elements, such as $\{a_0, a_1, \ldots\}$, will be denoted by $\{a_i\}$, $i = 0, 1, \ldots$, where needed.
$\alpha \in \mathbb{A}$	α is an element of $\mathbb{A}$.
N	An integer.
$\mathbb{A} \times \mathbb{B}$	Direct product of $\mathbb{A}$ and $\mathbb{B}$. It is the set $\{(x, y) \mid x \in \mathbb{A}, y \in \mathbb{Y}\}$.
$\mathbb{A}^2$	The set $\mathbb{A} \times \mathbb{A}$ with each element, called a 2-tuple, of the form $(\alpha \in \mathbb{A}, \beta \in \mathbb{A})$.
$\mathbb{A}^N$	For $N \geq 2$, the set $\mathbb{A} \times \mathbb{A}^{N-1}$ with $\mathbb{A}^1 = \mathbb{A}$. Each element, called an N-tuple, is of the form $(\alpha_0, \alpha_1, \ldots, \alpha_{N-1})$ with $\alpha_i \in \mathbb{A} \ \forall i$.

$\mathbb{Z}^N$	The set of positive integer N-tuples. Each element is a list of N positive integers.
$\mathbb{R}^N$	The set of real N-tuples. Each element is a list of N real numbers.
$\mathbb{R}^+$	The set of non-negative real numbers .
x	A scalar (element of $\mathbb{R}^1$ or $\mathbb{Z}^1$).
$\overline{x}$	A row vector $\overline{x} = (x_0, x_1, \ldots, x_{N-1})$ with $x_i \in \mathbb{R}^1$ or $x_i \in \mathbb{Z}^1$. If $x_i \in \mathbb{R}^1 \ \forall i$, $\overline{x} \in \mathbb{R}^N$ and if $x_i \in \mathbb{Z}^1 \ \forall i$, $\overline{x} \in \mathbb{Z}^N$.
$\|\overline{x}\|$	The norm of a vector.
$\mathbf{A}$	A matrix. The element of $\mathbf{A}$ in the ith row and j^{th} column is denoted by A_{ij}.
$\mathbf{A}^T$, $\overline{x}^T$	The transpose of $\mathbf{A}$ and $\overline{x}$ respectively.
X	A scalar random variable. It can be discrete or continuous.
$X \in \mathbb{A}$	The outcome of a trial gives a value of X in a set $\mathbb{A}$.
$\Pr(X \in \mathbb{A})$ or $\Pr(\mathbb{A})$	The probability of $X \in \mathbb{A}$.
$\overline{X}$	A vector random variable $\overline{X} = (X_0, X_1, \ldots, X_{N-1})$.
$P_X(x)$	The probability of a discrete random variable X having value x in a trial.
$p_X(x)$	The probability density function (pdf) of a continuous random variable X.
$p_{\overline{X}}(\overline{x})$	The joint pdf of $\overline{X}$.
$p_{\overline{X}|\overline{Y}}(\overline{x}|\overline{y})$	The conditional pdf of $\overline{X}$ given the trial value $\overline{y}$ of $\overline{Y}$.
$\min(a, b)$	The smaller of the two scalars a and b.
$\min_{\overline{x}} f(\overline{x})$	The minimum value of $f(\overline{x})$ over $\overline{x}$.
$\max_{\overline{x}} f(\overline{x})$	The maximum value of $f(\overline{x})$ over $\overline{x}$.
$\arg \min_{\overline{x}} f(\overline{x})$	The value of $\overline{x}$ at which $f(\overline{x})$ is minimum.

Introduction

CONTENTS

This chapter introduces the important role of optimization in statistical data analysis and provides an overview of the latter that, although not comprehensive, is adequate for the purpose of this book. Two concrete data analysis problems are described that constitute the testbeds used in this book for illustrating the application of swarm intelligence methods.

1.1 OPTIMIZATION IN STATISTICAL ANALYSIS

The objective of any kind of statistical analysis of given data is to consider a set of models for the process or phenomenon associated with the data and find the model that is best supported by it. This so-called *best-fit model* can then be used to make predictions about the phenomenon. The same idea figures prominently in the drive to develop computer algorithms in *machine learning* that can learn and generalize from examples.

Obtaining the best-fit model becomes a non-trivial task due to the presence of *randomness* (also called *noise* or *error*) – an unpredictable contaminant in the data. (When noise can be ignored, the analysis problem becomes one of *interpolation* or *function approximation*.) Due to this unpredictability, the theory of probability becomes the natural framework within which the methods of statistical analysis are derived. (See App. A for a brief review of some of the concepts in probability theory that are relevant to this book.)

The task of scanning across a given set of models to find the best-fit one is an optimization problem. Hence, optimization is at the core of statistical analysis as much as probability theory. Often, our choice of models is itself limited by the difficulty of the associated optimization problem. As our technology for handling optimization has evolved, mainly in terms of advances in computing and numerical algorithms, so has the type of models we are able to infer from data.

Another evolution in parallel, again enabled by advances in computing, has been in the technology for data collection that has resulted in very high data volumes and the era of *big data*. A large amount of data that is rich in information demands the use of models in its statistical analysis that are more flexible and, hence, have greater complexity. This, in turn, increases the difficulty of the optimization step.

Optimization problems arise in a wide array of fields, of course, and not just in statistical analysis. As such, a large variety of approaches have been and continue to be developed in diverse application domains. For the same reason, however, not all of them have found their way into the standard toolkit used in statistical analysis. Among the more recent ones are those based on emulating the behavior of biological swarms such as a flock of birds or an ant colony. It turns out that nature has figured out, through the blind process of evolution, that a swarm of cooperating entities, with each following a fairly simple set of behavioral rules, can solve difficult optimization problems. Optimization methods based on such approaches fall under the rubric of *swarm intelligence* (SI).

In this book, we will explore the use of SI methods in solving the optimization bottleneck that is often encountered in statistical analyses. Optimization methods that can handle difficult problems cannot, in general, be used as black-boxes: Some tuning of these methods is always needed in order to extract good performance from them. In the experience of the author, the best way to become familiar with this process is to implement SI methods on some concrete but realistic statistical analyses. This is the path followed in this book, where we focus on getting the reader started with some worked out examples that are simple enough to implement fairly easily but sufficiently complicated to mimic realistic problems.

1.2 STATISTICAL ANALYSIS: BRIEF OVERVIEW

A formal description of a statistical analysis problem is as follows. One is given trial values $\bar{z}_i$, $i = 0, 1, \ldots, N - 1$ of a vector random variable $\bar{Z}$ – the set $\mathbb{T} = \{\bar{z}_0, \bar{z}_1, \ldots, \bar{z}_{N-1}\}$ of trial values[1] is called a *data realization* (or just *data*) – and the goal is to consider a set of models for the joint probability density function (pdf), $p_{\bar{Z}}(\bar{z})$, of $\bar{Z}$ and find the one that is best supported by the data.

The task of obtaining this best-fit model is called *density estimation* . With the best-fit $p_{\bar{Z}}(\bar{z})$ in hand, one can make useful predictions or inferences about the phenomenon that generated the data. (While $\bar{z}_i$ can be a mixed combination of integers and real numbers in general, we restrict attention in the following to the case $\bar{z}_i \in \mathbb{R}^N$.)

Besides density estimation, statistical analysis also includes problems of *hypothesis testing*. In hypothesis testing, one has two competing sets of models for $p_{\bar{Z}}(\bar{z})$. The objective is to decide which of the two sets of models is best supported by the data. It is possible that each set itself contains more

---

[1]Alternatively denoted by $\{\bar{z}_i\}$, $i = 0, 1, \ldots, N - 1$.

than one model. So, the decision must take into account the variation of models within each set. We discuss hypothesis testing in further detail in Sec. 1.4.

Methods for density estimation can be divided, rather loosely, into *parametric* and *non-parametric* ones. This division is essentially based on how strong the assumptions embodied in the models of $p_{\overline{Z}}$ are *before* the data is obtained. If the set of models is prescribed independently of the data, we get a purely parametric method. If $p_{\overline{Z}}(\overline{z})$ is determined from the data itself without strong prior assumptions, we get a non-parametric method.

For example, deciding ahead of obtaining the data that $p_{\overline{Z}}(\overline{z})$ is a multivariate normal pdf (see App. A), with only its parameters, namely the mean vector and/or the covariance matrix, being unknown, yields an example of a parametric method. In contrast, inferring $p_{\overline{Z}}(\overline{z})$ by making a (possibly multi-dimensional) *histogram* is an example of a non-parametric method.

Strictly speaking, non-parametric methods are not parameter-free since they do contain parameters, such as the size and number of bins in the histogram example above. The main distinction is that the assumptions made about $p_{\overline{Z}}(\overline{z})$ are much weaker in the non-parametric approach. It is best to see parametric and non-parametric methods as lying at the extreme ends of a continuum of approaches in statistical analysis.

The appearance of the parameters is more explicit in parametric analysis. This is often shown by using $p_{\overline{Z}}(\overline{z}; \overline{\theta})$, where $\overline{\theta} = (\theta_0, \theta_1, \ldots, \theta_{P-1})$ is the set of parameters defining the models. For example, in the case of the multivariate normal pdf model (see Sec. A.6), $\overline{\theta}$ may include the vector of mean values, or the covariance matrix, or both.

A real-world example of a density estimation problem is finding groups in data consisting of the luminosity and temperature of some set of stars in our Galaxy. (We are talking here about the famous *Hertzsprung-Russell diagram* [50].) A parametric approach to the above problem could be based on using a *mixture model* where $p_{\overline{Z}}(\overline{z})$ is given by a superposition of prescribed (such as multivariate normal) pdfs. The fitting of mixture models to data is called *clustering* analysis. Clustering analysis can also be formulated in a non-parametric way.

In a subset of density estimation problems, the trial values are of a random vector of the form $\overline{Z} = (\overline{Y}, \overline{X})$, and the goal is to obtain the best-fit model for the conditional pdf $p_{\overline{Y}|\overline{X}}(\overline{y}|\overline{x})$. Such a problem is called a *statistical regression* problem and a model of $p_{\overline{Y}|\overline{X}}(\overline{y}|\overline{x})$ is called a *regression model*. $\overline{X}$ is called the *independent* and $\overline{Y}$ is called the *dependent* variable. The terminology in the literature on statistical analysis can vary a lot and, depending on the application area, the independent variable is also called *predictor, input,* or *feature*. Similarly, the dependent variable is also called *response, output,* or *outcome*. The set of regression models and the method used to find the best fit one among them constitute a *regression method*.

A simple example of a statistical regression problem is the prediction of temperature variation in a room during the course of a day. In this example, $z_i = (y_i, x_i)$, $i = 0, 1, \ldots, N - 1$, with $y_i \in \mathbb{R}^1$ being temperature and $x_i \in \mathbb{R}^1$ being the time at which y_i is measured. Statistical analysis provides a best fit model for $p_{Y|X}(y|x)$ and this model can be used to predict the temperature at a time instant x that does not belong to the set $\{x_0, x_1, \ldots, x_{N-1}\}$.

Another example is that of an image where $\overline{x}_i \in \mathbb{Z}^2$ is the location of a pixel in the image, while $y_i \in \mathbb{R}^1$ is the intensity of the recorded image at that pixel. For a colored digital image, $\overline{y}_i = (r_i, g_i, b_i) \in \mathbb{Z}^3$, where r_i, g_i, and b_i are the red, green, and blue intensities of the recorded image. The goal of statistical regression here could be to *denoise* the image: obtain a new image given by $E[\overline{Y}|\overline{X}]$, where the expectation is taken with respect to the best fit model of $p_{\overline{Y}|\overline{X}}(\overline{y}|\overline{x})$.

Statistical regression, being a subset of density estimation, also inherits parametric and non-parametric approaches. However, there is considerably more ambiguity in the literature on the distinction between the two as far as regression problems go. Non-parametric regression can also include the case of models that are parametric but have a large number of parameters that allow greater flexibility in capturing complexity in the data.

An important issue that arises in both parametric and non-parametric regression is that of *overfitting* where too many parameters can cause a model to adapt to every feature of the data, including the noise. Such a model then loses all predictive power because a small perturbation in the data can cause a significant change in the best fit model. Overfitting is an especially important issue for non-parametric regression since the models used are designed to be more adaptable to the data. The mitigation of overfitting requires the use of *model selection* and *regularization* techniques. Instances of these advanced topics will appear later on but they will not be covered in great depth in this book.

1.3 STATISTICAL REGRESSION

1.3.1 Parametric regression

In parametric regression, the set of models for $p_{\overline{Y}|\overline{X}}(\overline{y}|\overline{x})$ consists of functions that are labeled by a fixed number of parameters $\overline{\theta} = (\theta_0, \theta_1, \ldots, \theta_{P-1})$, where $\theta_i \in \mathbb{R}^1$ (or $\theta_i \in \mathbb{Z}^1$). As such, we can denote the conditional probability as $p_{\overline{Y}|\overline{X}}(\overline{y}|\overline{x}; \overline{\theta})$.

Consider the well-known example of fitting a straight line to a set $\mathbb{T} = \{(x_i \in \mathbb{R}^1, y_i \in \mathbb{R}^1)\}$, $i = 0, 1, \ldots, N-1$, of data points. In the simplest case, the regression model is $Y = f(X; \overline{\theta}) + E$, where $f(X; \overline{\theta}) = aX + b$, $\overline{\theta} = (a, b)$, and the error E is a normal random variable (see Sec. A.6) with zero mean and variance σ^2. (Error arising from X is a subtle issue that is briefly discussed in Sec. 1.5.1.) The conditional probability model is then given by

$$p_{Y|X}(y|x; \overline{\theta}) = p_E\left(y - f(x; \overline{\theta})\right) = N(y; ax + b, \sigma^2). \quad (1.1)$$

Now, let the conditional probability of obtaining the given data, $\mathbb{T}$, for a given $\overline{\theta}$ be denoted by $L(\mathbb{T}; \overline{\theta})$. For a fixed $\mathbb{T}$,

$L(\mathbb{T};\overline{\theta})$ considered as a function $\overline{\theta}$ is called the *likelihood function* of the data[2]. In the present case,

$$L(\mathbb{T};\overline{\theta}) \;=\; \Pi_{i=0}^{N-1} p_{\mathrm{E}}\left(y_i - f(x_i;\overline{\theta})\right) , \qquad (1.2)$$

$$\propto\; \exp\left(-\frac{1}{2\sigma^2}\sum_{i=0}^{N-1}(y_i - ax_i - b)^2\right) . \qquad (1.3)$$

In the *Maximum Likelihood Estimation* (MLE) method, the best-fit model is obtained by maximizing the likelihood function over the model parameters $\overline{\theta}$. Since the exponential function depends monotonically on its argument, maximimization of $L(\mathbb{T};\overline{\theta})$ is equivalent to maximizing the exponent (i.e., its natural logarithm), or (since the exponent is negative) minimizing

$$L_S(\mathbb{T};\overline{\theta}) = \frac{1}{2\sigma^2}\sum_{i=0}^{N-1}\left(y_i - f(x_i;\overline{\theta})\right)^2 . \qquad (1.4)$$

over $\overline{\theta}$. Most readers will recognize $L_S(\mathbb{T};\overline{\theta})$ – barring the unimportant constant factor $1/(2\sigma^2)$ – as the *sum of squared residuals* that is used in *least squares* fitting of a straight line to a set of points. From here on, therefore, we will call L_S the *least squares function*.

The minimization problem above illustrates the role of optimization in statistical regression. It is straightforward to do the optimization analytically in the straight line fitting problem because the parameters appear linearly in the regression model, making $L_S(\mathbb{T};\overline{\theta})$ a simple quadratic function of the parameters. In general, however, the optimization problem is not trivial if the parameters appear non-linearly in the regression model. The only option then is to optimize the likelihood numerically.

In this book, we will use the following non-linear model when discussing the application of SI methods to parametric regression.

---

[2]Note that the likelihood function could have been introduced in the discussion of density estimation itself. However, we prefer to do so here because our focus in this book is only on statistical regression.

Quadratic chirp in iid noise:

$$Y = q_c(X; \bar{\theta}) + E, \qquad (1.5)$$

where

$$q_c(X) = A\sin(2\pi\phi(X)), \qquad (1.6)$$
$$\phi(X) = a_1 X + a_2 X^2 + a_3 X^3. \qquad (1.7)$$

There are 4 parameters in this model $\bar{\theta} = (A, a_1, a_2, a_3)$. (For clarity in notation, $\bar{\theta}$ is dropped when there is no scope for confusion.) Fig. 1.1 shows an example of $q_c(X)$ and a data realization for regularly spaced values of X.

As before (c.f., Eq. 1.4), the maximization of the likelihood reduces to the minimization of

$$L_S(\mathbb{T}; \bar{\theta}) = \frac{1}{2\sigma^2} \sum_{i=0}^{N-1} (y_i - q_c(x_i))^2. \qquad (1.8)$$

As we will see later in Sec. 5.1.1, the minimization of $L_S(\mathbb{T}; \bar{\theta})$ over A can be performed analytically, leaving behind a function that must be minimized numerically over the remaining three parameters.

1.3.2 Non-parametric regression

In non-parametric regression problems, no explicit assumption is made about the functional form of models for $p_{\overline{Y}|\overline{X}}(\bar{y}|\bar{x})$. Instead, the assumptions made are about some global properties of the models. For example, one may assume that $f(\overline{X}) = E[\overline{Y}|\overline{X}]$, the conditional expectation of $\overline{Y}$ given $\overline{X}$, is a "smooth" function in the sense that its derivatives exist up to a prescribed order. In other cases, one may forgo smoothness but impose a property such as positivity on $f(\overline{X})$.

Another approach in non-parametric regression problems is to adopt a functional form for $p_{\overline{Y}|\overline{X}}(\bar{y}|\bar{x})$ but keep the set of parameters sufficiently large such that the functional form is very flexible. Since having too much flexibility can lead to

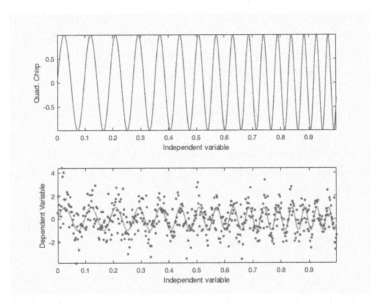

Figure 1.1 The top panel shows a quadratic chirp $q_c(\mathrm{X})$, defined in Eqs. 1.6 and 1.7, for equally spaced values of X with $x_i = i\Delta$, $\Delta = 1/512$, and $i = 0, 1, \ldots, 511$. The parameter values are $A = 1$, $a_1 = 10$, and $a_2 = a_3 = 3$. The bottom panel shows a data realization $\{(x_i, y_i)\}$, $i = 0, 1, \ldots, 511$, following the model given in Eq. 1.5.

a model that offers a very good fit but only to the given data, namely an overfitted model, additional constraints are imposed that restrict the choice of parameter values.

We will illustrate the application of SI methods to non-parametric regression problems through the following example.

Spline-based smoothing:

The regression model is $Y = f(X) + E$, where $f(X)$ is only assumed to be a smooth, but an otherwise unknown, function. One way to implement smoothness is to require that the average squared curvature of $f(X)$, defined as

$$\frac{1}{(b-a)} \int_a^b dx \left(\frac{d^2 f}{dx^2}\right)^2 , \qquad (1.9)$$

for $x \in [a, b]$ be sufficiently small. It can be shown that the best least-squares estimate of $f(X)$ under this requirement must be a *cubic spline*. (See App. B for a bare-bones review of splines and the associated terminology.)

Thus, we will assume $f(X)$ to be a cubic spline defined by a set of M *breakpoints* denoted by $\bar{b} = (b_0, b_1, \ldots, b_{M-1})$, where $b_{i+1} > b_i$. The set of all cubic splines defined by the same $\bar{b}$ is a linear vector space. One of the basis sets of this vector space is that of *B-spline* functions $B_{j,4}(x; \bar{b})$, $j = 0, 1, \ldots, M - 1$. (It is assumed here that the cubic splines decay to zero at $X = b_0$ and $X = b_{M-1}$.) It follows that $f(X)$ is a linear combination of the B-splines given by

$$f(X) = \sum_{j=0}^{M-1} \alpha_j B_{j,4}(X; \bar{b}) , \qquad (1.10)$$

where $\bar{\alpha} = (\alpha_0, \alpha_1, \ldots, \alpha_{M-1})$ is the set of coefficients in the linear combination.

Finding the best-fit model here involves finding the values of $\bar{\theta} = (\bar{\alpha}, \bar{b})$ for which the least-squares function

$$L_S(\mathbb{T}; \bar{\theta}) = \frac{1}{2\sigma^2} \sum_{i=0}^{N-1} \left(y_i - \sum_{j=0}^{M-1} \alpha_j B_{j,4}(X; \bar{b})\right)^2 , \qquad (1.11)$$

is minimized. If $\bar{b}$ is fixed, the coefficients $\bar{\alpha}$ can be found easily since, as in the case of the straight line fitting problem, they appear quadratically in the least-squares function. The regression method based on this approach is called *spline smoothing*.

However, if $\bar{b}$ is allowed to vary, then the minimization problem cannot be solved analytically alone and numerical methods must be used. Varying the breakpoints in order to find the best fit spline is called *knot optimization* (See App. B for the distinction between knots and breakpoints) and the corresponding regression method is called *regression spline*. It is known [24] to provide a better fitting model than spline smoothing but it is also an extremely challenging optimization problem that has prevented its use from becoming more widespread. Various approaches have been devised to tackle this problem[3] but it is only recently that SI methods have begun to be explored (e.g., [17]) for this interesting problem.

To test the performance of the regression spline method, we will use data where

$$f(X) \propto B_{0,4}(X; \bar{c}) , \qquad (1.12)$$

namely, a single B-spline function defined by breakpoints $\bar{c}$. The values of X are confined to $[0, 1]$ and $\bar{c} = (0.3, 0.4, 0.45, 0.5, 0.55)$. Fig. 1.2 shows examples of both the $f(X)$ defined above and the data.

1.4 HYPOTHESES TESTING

As discussed above, statistical regression is a special case of the more general density estimation problem where one has to obtain the best fit among a set of models for the joint pdf $p_{\overline{Z}}(\bar{z})$ of data $\bar{z}$.

A different statistical analysis problem, that of hypotheses testing, is concerned with deciding which among two sets of

---

[3]A good entry point for the literature on this subject is the journal *Computer-Aided Design.*

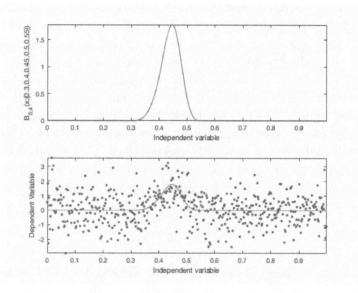

Figure 1.2 The top panel shows the function $f(\mathrm{X})$ in Eq. 1.12 that is used for generating test data for the regression spline method. Here, X is equally spaced with $x_i = i\Delta$, $\Delta = 1/512$, and $i = 0, 1, \ldots, 511$, and $f(\mathrm{X}) = 10B_{0,4}(x; \bar{c})$, with $\bar{c} = (0.3, 0.4, 0.45, 0.5, 0.55)$. The bottom panel shows a data realization.

models best explains the data. The new element of making a decision in the presence of noise leads to two types of errors, called *false alarm* and *false dismissal*, that are absent in density estimation. The theory behind hypotheses testing is an elaborate subject in itself and lies outside the scope of this book. However, it will suffice here to discuss just a few of the main results from this theory.

One is that it is possible to come up with a "best" test in the special case of *binary hypotheses* where there are only two competing models to choose from. An example is when we have two models, $Y = E$ and $Y = f(X) + E$, with $f(X)$ a known function, and a choice needs to be made between the two models. Traditionally, the two models are respectively called the H_0 or *null hypothesis*, and the H_1 or *alternative hypothesis*. The joint pdf of the data under H_i, $i = 0, 1$, is denoted by $p_{\overline{Z}}(\overline{z}|H_i)$.

Deciding on H_1 (H_0) when the true hypothesis is H_0 (H_1) leads to a false alarm (false dismissal) error. Under the *Neyman-Pearson* criterion [31], the best test for a binary hypotheses is the one that minimizes the false dismissal probability for a given probability of false alarm. The test consists of computing the *log-likelihood ratio* (L_R) of the data,

$$
L_R = \ln\left(\frac{p_{\overline{Z}}(\overline{z}|H_1)}{p_{\overline{Z}}(\overline{z}|H_0)}\right), \tag{1.13}
$$

and comparing L_R to a threshold value η (called the *detection threshold*): H_1 is selected if $L_R \geq \eta$, and H_0 otherwise.

Note that L_R is a random variable because of noise in the data $\overline{z}$. Depending on which hypothesis is the true one, its pdf is $p_{L_R}(x|H_i)$. The detection threshold is fixed once a false alarm probability, P_{FP}, given by

$$
P_{\text{FP}} = \int_{\eta}^{\infty} dx \, p_{L_R}(x|H_0), \tag{1.14}
$$

for the test is specified.

A scenario that is closer to real-world problems than the binary hypothesis test, is that of a *composite hypotheses* test. An example is when we have two sets of models, H_0 : $Y = E$ and H_1 : $Y = f(X; \bar{\theta}) + E$, where $f(X; \bar{\theta})$ is a function parameterized by $\bar{\theta}$ (such as the quadratic chirp with $\bar{\theta} = (A, a_1, a_2, a_3)$) but the true value of $\bar{\theta}$ is unknown. Here, the set of models under H_1 has many models in it while the set of models under H_0 has just one. In the general case, the joint pdf of the data under H_1 is $p_{\bar{Z}}(\bar{z}|H_1; \bar{\theta})$, where $\bar{\theta}$ is unknown. (Here, $\bar{\theta}$ should be seen as a label for models and, hence, includes the case of non-parametric regression also.)

The theory of hypotheses testing tells us that there is no best test, except in some trivial cases, that can minimize the false dismissal probability across all values of $\bar{\theta}$ for a given P_{FP}. However, it is found quite often that a straightforward generalization of the log-likelihood ratio test, called the *Generalized Likelihood Ratio Test* (GLRT), gives a good performance. The GLRT requires that we compute a quantity L_G, given by

$$L_G = \max_{\bar{\theta}} \ln \left(\frac{p_{\bar{Z}}(\bar{z}|H_1; \bar{\theta})}{p_{\bar{Z}}(\bar{z}|H_0)} \right) , \qquad (1.15)$$

and compare it to a detection threshold. As before, H_1 is selected if L_G exceeds the threshold.

For a regression problem where $\bar{Z} = (\bar{Y}, \bar{X})$, $\bar{X}$ and $\bar{Y}$ being the independent and dependent variables respectively, we get

$$L_G = \max_{\bar{\theta}} \ln \left(\frac{p_{\bar{Y}|\bar{X}}(\bar{y}|\bar{x}; H_1, \bar{\theta})}{p_{\bar{Y}|\bar{X}}(\bar{y}|\bar{x}; H_0)} \right) . \qquad (1.16)$$

Note that, since $\bar{\theta}$ is absent in $p_{\bar{Y}|\bar{X}}(\bar{y}|\bar{x}; H_0)$, the maximimization over $\bar{\theta}$ in Eq. 1.16 is only over $p_{\bar{Y}|\bar{X}}(\bar{y}|\bar{x}; H_1, \bar{\theta})$. This is nothing but the likelihood function introduced in Sec. 1.3.1. Thus, GLRT is closely linked to statistical regression.

The general form of the GLRT for the examples in Secs. 1.3.1 and 1.3.2 is,

$$L_G = \min_{\bar{\theta}} L_S(\mathbb{T}; \bar{\theta}) - \frac{1}{2\sigma^2} \sum_{i=0}^{N-1} y_i^2 , \qquad (1.17)$$

where $\bar{\theta}$ denotes the respective parameters. Thus, L_G in these examples is obtained in a straightforward manner from the global minimum of the least squares function.

1.5 NOTES

The brevity of the overview of statistical analysis presented in this chapter demands incompleteness in many important respects. Topics such as the specification of errors in parameter estimation and obtaining confidence intervals instead of point estimates are some of the important omissions. Also omitted are some of the important results in the theoretical foundations of statistics, such as the Cramer-Rao lower bound on estimation errors and the RBLS theorem.

While the overview, despite these omissions, is adequate for the rest of the book, the reader will greatly benefit from perusing textbooks such as [26, 25, 15] for a firmer foundation in statistical analysis. Much of the material in this chapter is culled from these books. Non-parametric smoothing methods, including spline smoothing, are covered in detail in [20].

Some important topics that were touched upon only briefly in this chapter are elaborated upon a little more below.

1.5.1 Noise in the independent variable

In the examples illustrating statistical regression in Sec. 1.2, one may object to treating the independent variable, $\overline{X}$, as random. After all, we think of a quantity such as the time instant at which the temperature of a room is measured as being completely under our control and not the trial outcome of a random variable.

The nature of the independent variable – random or not – is actually immaterial to a statistical regression problem since one is only interested in the conditional probability $p_{\overline{Y}|\overline{X}}$, where the value of $\overline{X}$ is a given.

That said, one must remember that even the independent variable in real data is the outcome of some measurement and, hence, has error in it. For example, time is measured using a clock and no clock is perfect. Usually, this error is negligible and can be ignored compared to the error in the measurement of the dependent variable. Problems where the error in the independent variable is not negligible are called *errors-in-variables* regression problems. The Wikipedia entry [49] on this topic is a good starting point for further exploration.

1.5.2 Statistical analysis and machine learning

The advent of computers has led to a dramatic evolution of statistical methodology. Some methods, such as *Bootstrapping* [13], are purely a result of merging statistics with computing. At the same time, it is now widely accepted that the probabilistic framework underlying statistical analysis is also fruitful in advancing a holy grail of computing, namely the creation of machines that can learn like humans from experience and apply this learning to novel situations. Thus, there is a strong overlap between the concepts and methods in the fields of statistical analysis and *machine learning*. However, due to their different origins and historical development, there is a considerable divergence in the terminology used in the two fields for essentially the same concepts.

In the machine learning literature, the task of obtaining the best-fit model is called *learning*, density estimation is called *unsupervised learning*, and statistical regression is called *supervised learning*. The data provided in a supervised learning problem is called *training data*.

The main difference between statistical regression and machine learning is that the element of randomness is mainly localized in the dependent variable, $\overline{Y}$, in the former while it is predominantly in the independent variable, $\overline{X}$, for the latter. This is because instances of X, such as images, are obtained from generic sources, such as the web, without a fine degree of control.

The emphasis in machine learning is on obtaining a best fit model for the joint pdf of data from a training data set such that the model generalizes well to new data. Since the typical applications of machine learning, such as object recognition in images or the recognition of spoken words, involve inherently complicated models for the joint pdf, a large amount of training data is required for successful learning. This requirement has dovetailed nicely with the emergence of big data, which has led to the availability of massive amounts of training data related to real world tasks. It is no surprise, therefore, that the field of machine learning has seen breathtaking advances recently.

Deeper discussions of the overlap between statistical and machine learning concepts can be found in [15, 19].

Stochastic Optimization Theory

CONTENTS

This chapter touches upon some of the principal results from optimization theory that have a bearing on swarm intelligence methods. After establishing the terminology used to describe optimization problems in general, the two main classes of these problems are discussed that determine the types of optimization methods – deterministic or stochastic – that can be used. Some general results pertaining to stochastic optimization methods are outlined that set the boundaries for their performance. This is followed by a description of the metrics used in the characterization and comparison of stochastic optimization methods. A simple strategy is described for extracting better performance from stochastic optimization methods that is well-suited to parallel computing.

2.1 TERMINOLOGY

The objective in an optimization problem is to find the optimum (maximum or minimum) value of a *fitness function* $f(\overline{x})$, $\overline{x} \in \mathbb{D} \subseteq \mathbb{R}^D$. The subset $\mathbb{D}$ is called the *search space* for the optimization problem and D is the *dimensionality* of the search space. Alternative terms used in the literature are *objective function* and *constraint space* (or *feasible set*) for the fitness function and search space respectively. (Strictly speaking, the above definition is that of a *continuous optimization* problem. We do not consider *discrete* or combinatorial optizimation problems, where $\overline{x} \in \mathbb{Z}^D$, in this book.)

The location, denoted as $\overline{x}^*$ below, of the optimum is called the *optimizer* (*maximizer* or *minimizer* depending on the type of optimization problem). Since finding the maximizer of a fitness function $f(\overline{x})$ is completely equivalent to finding the minimizer of $-f(\overline{x})$, we only consider minimization problems in the following.

Formally stated, a minimization problem consists of solving for $\overline{x}^*$ such that

$$f(\overline{x}^*) \ \leq \ f(\overline{x}) \,, \forall \overline{x} \in \mathbb{D} \,. \tag{2.1}$$

Equivalently,

$$f(\overline{x}^*) \ = \ \min_{\overline{x} \in \mathbb{D}} f(\overline{x}) \,. \tag{2.2}$$

This is stated more directly as,

$$\overline{x}^* \ = \ \arg \min_{\overline{x} \in \mathbb{D}} f(\overline{x}) \,. \tag{2.3}$$

Note that the minimizer of a function need not be a unique point. A simple counterexample is a fitness function that has a constant value over $\mathbb{D}$. Then all $\overline{x} \in \mathbb{D}$ are minimizers of the fitness function.

One can classify a minimizer further as a *local minimizer* or a *global minimizer*. The corresponding values of the fitness function are the *local minimum* and *global minimum* respectively. The definition of a minimizer given above is that of the global minimizer over $\mathbb{D}$. If $f(\overline{x})$ is differentiable and its gradient

$$\bigtriangledown f(\overline{x}) = \left(\frac{\partial f}{\partial x_0}, \frac{\partial f}{\partial x_1}, \ldots, \frac{\partial f}{\partial x_{N-1}} \right) , \quad (2.4)$$

vanishes ($\bigtriangledown f = (0, 0, \ldots, 0)$) at $\overline{x}^*$, then $\overline{x}^*$ is a local minimizer. Formally, a local minimizer is the global minimizer but over an open subset of the search space. A local minimizer may also be the global minimizer over the whole search space but this need not be true in general.

In this chapter, the following functions serve as concrete examples of fitness functions.

Generalized Rastrigin:

$$f(\overline{x}) = \sum_{i=1}^{D} \left[x_i^2 - 10\cos(2\pi x_i) + 10 \right] . \quad (2.5)$$

Generalized Griewank:

$$f(\overline{x}) = \frac{1}{4000} \sum_{i=1}^{D} x_i^2 - \prod_{i=1}^{D} \cos\left(\frac{x_i}{\sqrt{i}} \right) + 1 . \quad (2.6)$$

Fig. 2.1 shows the generalized Rastrigin function for $D = 2$. The global minimizer of this function is the origin $\overline{x}^* = (0, 0, \ldots, 0)$. The function also exhibits numerous local minima. Here, the global minimizer is also a local one.

2.2 CONVEX AND NON-CONVEX OPTIMIZATION PROBLEMS

A set $\mathbb{D} \subset \mathbb{R}^D$ is said to be a *convex set* if for any two elements $\overline{a}, \overline{b} \in \mathbb{D}$ and $0 < \lambda < 1$, the element $\overline{c} = (1 - \lambda)\overline{a} + \lambda\overline{b}$ also belongs to $\mathbb{D}$. In other words, all the points on the straight line joining any two points in $\mathbb{D}$ also lie within $\mathbb{D}$. As an example, the points constituting an elliptical area in a two dimensional plane form a convex set.

Consider a function $f(\overline{x})$ with $\overline{x} \in \mathbb{D} \subset \mathbb{R}^D$. As illustrated in Fig. 2.1 for the $D = 2$ case, the function defines a "surface"

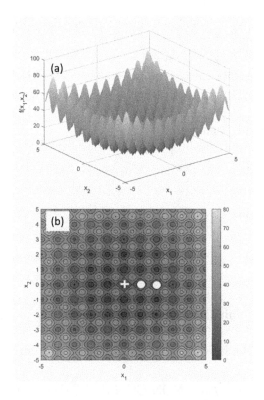

Figure 2.1 (a) The generalized Rastrigin function for a 2-dimensional search space, and (b) its contour plot showing the global ('+') and some local ('○') minimizers.

over $\mathbb{D}$. Taking all the points above this surface yields a "volume" in $D + 1$ dimensional space. If this volume is convex, then the function surface is said to be convex. The formal definition goes as follows: Take the subset $\mathbb{D}_f$ of the Cartesian product set $\mathbb{D} \times \mathbb{R}$ such that for each element $(\overline{x}, y) \in \mathbb{D}_f$, $\overline{x} \in \mathbb{D}$ and $y \geq f(\overline{x})$. If $\mathbb{D}_f$ is convex, then $f(\overline{x})$ is a convex function. While we skip the formal proof here, it is easy to convince oneself that the definition of convexity of a function implies that $f((1 - \lambda)\overline{a} + \lambda\overline{b}) \leq (1 - \lambda)f(\overline{a}) + \lambda f(\overline{b})$. This inequality is an alternative definition of a convex function.

One of the principal theorems in optimization theory states that the global minimum of a convex function $f(\overline{x})$ over a convex set $\mathbb{D}$ is also a local minimum and that there is only one local minimum. A *non-convex* function, on the other hand, can have multiple local minima in the search space and the global minimum need not coincide with any of the local minima. The Rastrigin function is an example of a non-convex fitness function. The optimization of a non-convex function is a *non-convex optimization* problem.

The local minimizer of a convex function can be found using the *method of steepest descent*: step along a sequence of points in the search space such that at each point, the step to the next point is directed opposite to the gradient of the fitness function at that point. Since the gradient at the local minimizer vanishes, the method will terminate once it hits the local minimizer. Steepest descent is an example of a *deterministic optimization* method since the same starting point and step size always results in the same path to the local minimizer.

For a non-convex optimization problem, the method of steepest descent will only take us to some local minimizer. When the local minima are spaced closely, steepest descent will not move very far from its starting point before it hits a local minimizer and terminates. Thus, steepest descent or any similar deterministic optimization method is not useful for locating the global minimizer in a non-convex optimization problem.

Before proceeding further, we caution the reader that the description of steepest descent just presented is very simplistic. In reality, much more sophistication is required in the choice of step sizes and other parameters. However, since we do not dwell on local minimization further in this book, the simple description above is appropriate for our purpose.

2.3 STOCHASTIC OPTIMIZATION

The only deterministic method to find the global optimum in a non-convex optimization problem is to set up a grid of points in the search space, evaluate the fitness function at each point, and interpolate these values to find the minimum fitness value. While this is a reasonable approach in low-dimensional search spaces (2 to 3), it is easy to see that it is a poor strategy as the dimensionality grows.

Take the simple case of a fixed number, N_G, of grid locations along each dimension. Then the total number of grid points throughout a search space grows exponentially fast, as N_G^D, with the dimensionality, D, of the search space. As an example, with $N_G = 100$, the total number of points goes up to 10^{10} even with a modest dimensionality of $D = 5$.

Even with smarter grid-based search strategies, it is practically impossible to avoid the exponential explosion in the number of points with the dimensionality of a search space. In general, all deterministic global minimization methods, which are all variations of a grid-based search, become computationally infeasible quite rapidly even in problems with moderate search space dimensionalities.

Given the infeasibility of deterministic methods for non-convex optimization, almost every method proposed to solve this problem involves some element of randomness. Such a method, which we call a *stochastic optimization* method, evaluates the fitness at points that are trial outcomes of a random vector. The element of randomness in the search strategy is a critical ingredient because it allows a stochastic optimization method to avoid getting trapped by local minimizers. (There also exist stochastic local minimization methods, but we do not consider them here.)

It is best to clarify here that, in the literature, stochastic optimization also refers to the optimization of stochastic functions using methods such as *stochastic approximation.* While the fitness functions in statistical regression are indeed stochastic, since the underlying data is a realization from a joint pdf, this book only considers the more restricted definition where a stochastic optimization method is applied to a deterministic function.

There exists a mathematical framework [44] that includes most stochastic optimization methods as special instances of a general method. The reader may wish to peruse App. A for a brief review of probability theory and associated notation before proceeding further.

General stochastic optimization method: An iterative algorithm where $\bar{x}[k]$ is the candidate position of the minimizer at step $k \in \mathbb{Z}^1$.

- *Initialization*: Set $k = 0$ and draw $\bar{x}[0] \in \mathbb{D} \subset \mathbb{R}^D$, where $\mathbb{D}$ is the search space. Normally, $\bar{x}[0]$ is drawn from a specified joint pdf, an example of which is provided later.

- Repeat

  - *Randomization*: Draw a trial value $\bar{v}[k] \in \mathbb{R}^D$ of a vector random variable $\overline{V} = (V_0, V_1, \ldots, V_{D-1})$ with a joint pdf $p_{\overline{V}}(\bar{x}; k)$. (The dependence on k means that the pdf can change form as the iterations progress.)

  - *Update position*: $\bar{x}[k+1] = A(\bar{x}[k], \bar{v}[k])$, which indicates that the new position is some prescribed function of the old position and $\bar{v}[k]$. The range of the function should be $\mathbb{D}$, ensuring that the new position stays within the search space.

  - *Update pdf*: $p_{\overline{V}}(\bar{x}; k) \rightarrow p_{\overline{V}}(\bar{x}; k+1)$.

  - Increment k to $k+1$.

- Until a *termination* condition becomes true. The simplest termination condition is to stop after a preset number of iterations are completed, but more sophisticated alternatives are also possible.

Different stochastic optimization algorithms correspond to different choices for $p_{\overline{V}}(\overline{x}; k)$, $A(\overline{x}, \overline{y})$ and the update rule for $p_{\overline{V}}(\overline{x}; k)$. It is important to emphasize here that each of these components can contain a set of more elaborate operations. For example, the trial value of $\overline{V}$ could itself be the result of combining the trial values of a larger set of random vectors and the set of fitness values found in past iterations.

Since a stochastic optimization algorithm, by definition, does not have a predictable terminal location in the search space, success for such algorithms must be defined in probabilistic terms. One cannot define success as the probability of $\overline{x}[k] = \overline{x}^*$ because $\overline{x}[k]$ is the trial value of a continuous vector random variable and the probability that it takes an exact value is zero (see App. A). However, it is legitimate to ask if $\overline{x}[k]$ falls in some volume, no matter how small, containing $\overline{x}^*$.

Formally, one defines an *optimality region*, for a given $\epsilon > 0$, as the set $\mathbb{R}_\epsilon = \{\overline{x} \in \mathbb{D} | f(\overline{x}) \leq f(\overline{x}^*) + \epsilon\}$. A stochastic algorithm is said to converge to the global minimum if

$$\lim_{k \to \infty} P(\overline{x}[k] \in \mathbb{R}_\epsilon) = 1. \tag{2.7}$$

That is, the probability of the final solution landing in the optimality region goes to unity asymptotically with the number of iterations.

The following conditions are sufficient for the general stochastic optimization method to converge.

- **Algorithm condition**: The fitness value always improves; $f(\overline{x}[k + 1]) \leq f(\overline{x}[k])$ and if $\overline{v}[k] \in \mathbb{D}$, $f(\overline{x}[k + 1]) \leq f(\overline{v}[k])$.

- **Convergence condition**: There is no region of the search space that the random vector, $\overline{V}$, does not visit at least once. Equivalently, for any given region $\mathbb{S} \subset \mathbb{D}$, the probability of not getting a trial value $\overline{v}[k]$ in $\mathbb{S}$ diminishes to zero as the iterations progress; $\prod_{k=0}^{\infty} (1 - P(\overline{v}[k] \in \mathbb{S})) = 0$.

Unfortunately, these two conditions work against each other: On one hand, the method must keep descending to lower fitness values but on the other, it should also examine every little region of the search space no matter how small. It is remarkable, therefore, that it is at all possible to come up with stochastic optimization methods that satisfy these conditions.

One such algorithm is "Algorithm 3" of [44]) that is defined as follows. (a) The position update rule is simply

$$A(\overline{x}, \overline{y}) = \begin{cases} \overline{y}, & f(\overline{y}) < f(\overline{x}), \\ \overline{x}, & \text{otherwise} \end{cases} . \qquad (2.8)$$

(b) In the randomization step, the trial value $\overline{v}[k]$ of the vector random variable $\overline{V}$ is obtained as follows. First, a trial value $\overline{w}$ is drawn for a vector random variable $\overline{W}$ that has a uniform joint pdf over $\mathbb{D}$: This means that $P(\overline{w} \in \mathbb{S} \subset \mathbb{D}) = \mu(\mathbb{S})/\mu(\mathbb{D})$ for any $\mathbb{S} \subset \mathbb{D}$, where $\mu(\mathbb{A})$ denotes the volume of $\mathbb{A}$. Then, a local minimization method is started at $\overline{w}$. The location returned by the local minimization is $\overline{v}[k]$. (c) The pdf $p_{\overline{V}}$ from which $\overline{v}[k]$ is drawn is determined implicitly by the procedure in (b) above. (c) The algorithm is initialized by drawing $\overline{x}[0]$ from the same joint pdf as that of $\overline{W}$.

While guaranteed to converge in the limit of infinite iterations, the above algorithm is not a practical one. First, since the number of iterations must always be finite in practice, convergence need not happen. Secondly, the computational cost of evaluating the fitness function is an important consideration in the total number of iterations that can be performed. This often requires moving the number of iterations towards as few as possible, a diametrically opposite condition to the one above for convergence. Shortening the number of iterations necessarily means that an algorithm will not be able to visit every region of the search space.

Thus, practical stochastic optimization algorithms can never be guaranteed to converge in a finite number of iterations. Different methods will have different probabilities of landing in the optimality region, and this probability, which depends on a complicated interaction between the algorithm and the fitness function, is usually difficult to compute.

In fact, the *no free lunch* (NFL) theorem in optimization theory [52] tells us that there is no magic stochastic optimization method that has the best performance across all optimization problems. More precisely, the NFL theorem states that, averaged across all fitness functions, the performance of one stochastic optimization method is as good as any other. In particular, this means that there is an infinity of fitness functions over which a pure random search is better than any other more sophisticated optimization method (and vice versa)! That said, the NFL theorem does not prevent one stochastic optimization method from being the best over a suitably restricted class of fitness functions.

2.4 EXPLORATION AND EXPLOITATION

While the sufficiency conditions for convergence are not satisfied by most practical stochastic optimization methods, they serve to lay out the type of behavior a method must have in order to be useful. The convergence condition entails that a stochastic optimization method should spend some fraction of iterations in exploring the search space before finding a candidate optimality region for a deeper search using the remaining iterations. These two phases are generally called *exploration* and *exploitation*. During both of these phases, the algorithm must continue to descend the fitness function in keeping with the algorithm condition.

The relative lengths of the exploration and exploitation phases that an optimization method should have depend, among other factors, on the degree to which the local minima of a fitness function are crowded together, a property that is often called *ruggedness*, and the dimensionality of the search space. Too short an exploration phase can lead to convergence to a local minima rather than the global minimum. Too long an exploration phase, on the other hand, increases the computational cost of the optimization.

The effect of the dimensionality of the search space on the exploration behavior of an optimization method can be particularly counter-intuitive. Consider the initialization step for a stochastic optimization method and let us assume that the initial location is obtained from a uniform pdf over the search space. For simplicity, let the search space be a cube in D-dimensions (a *hypercube*) with side length b in each dimension. This means that each component x_i, $i = 0, 1, \ldots, D$, of the position vector $\bar{x} \in \mathbb{D}$ can vary independently in an interval $[a_i, a_i + b]$. (A more general definition of a hypercube is that $x_i \in [a_i, b_i]$, $b_i - a_i > 0$.)

Given that the pdf is uniform over the search space, our intuition built on low-dimensional examples, such as the uniform pdf over the real line, would suggest that the fraction of trials in which the initial location falls around the center of the cube is the same or more than that around a point near the boundary. However, this is not so: the volume contained in an inner cube of side length $a < b$ around the center, which is a^D, decreases exponentially relative to the volume $b^D - a^D$ in the rest of the cube. Hence, most of the initial locations will actually be quite far from the center.

For example, for $a = 0.9b$, the ratio of the inner and outer volumes for $D = 2$ is 2.7, showing that most of the volume is occupied by the inner cube, but it is only 0.14 when $D = 20$! Thus, even though the inner cube sides are nearly as big as those of the outer cube, most of the volume in the latter is near its walls. Counter-intuitive effects like this in higher dimensions are clubbed together under the term *curse of dimensionality*. Due to such effects, stochastic optimization methods that shorten exploration relative to exploitation may work well and converge quickly in low dimensional search spaces but fail miserably as the dimensionality grows.

In order to be a practical and useful tool, it should be easy for the user of a stochastic optimization method to control the relative lengths of the exploration and exploitation phases. If the algorithm has a large number of parameters whose influence on these two phases is obscure and difficult to disentangle, it becomes very difficult for a non-expert user to set these parameters for achieving success in a real-world problem.

2.5 BENCHMARKING

Since stochastic optimization methods are neither guaranteed to converge nor perform equally well across all possible fitness functions, it is extremely important to test a given stochastic optimization method across a sufficiently diverse suite of fitness functions to gauge the limits of its performance. This process is called *benchmarking*.

Any measure of the performance of a stochastic optimization method on a given fitness function is bound to be a random variable. Hence, benchmarking and the comparison of different methods must employ a statistical approach. This requires running a given method on not only a sufficiently diverse set of fitness functions but also running it multiple times on each one. The initialization of the method and the sequence of random numbers should be statistically independent across the runs.

To keep the computational cost of doing the resulting large number of fitness function evaluations manageable, the fitness functions used for benchmarking must be computationally inexpensive to evaluate. At the same time, these functions should provide enough of a challenge to the optimization methods if benchmarking is to be useful. In particular, the fitness functions should be extensible to an arbitrary number of search space dimensions. Several such benchmark fitness functions have been developed in the literature and an extensive list can be found in Table I of [4]. The Rastrigin and Griewank functions introduced earlier in Eq. 2.5 and Eq. 2.6 are in fact two such benchmark fitness functions.

Comparisons of optimization methods based on benchmark fitness functions should not only look at the final fitness value found but also their exploration-exploitation trade-off. The following is a standard method that is often adopted in the literature in this context.

For each method, multiple runs are carried out on a given fitness function and the fitness value at each iteration for each run are recorded. Let the sequence of fitness values obtained at each iteration step be denoted by $\overline{f}^{(i)}$ for the ith independent run. Then

$$\overline{f}^{(\text{av})} = \frac{1}{N_{\text{runs}}} \sum_{i=1}^{N_{\text{runs}}} \overline{f}^{(i)}, \qquad (2.9)$$

is the sequence of average fitness values found by the optimization method as a function of the number of elapsed iterations. Since the actual number of fitness function evaluations made at each iteration step depends on the details of the optimization algorithm, $\overline{f}^{(\text{av})}$ is often shown as a function of the number of fitness evaluations rather than the number of iterations. This leads to a fairer comparison of optimization methods because the computational cost of algorithms is often one of the prime considerations when deciding which one to use.

Fig. 2.2 shows examples of $\overline{f}^{(\text{av})}$ and illustrates several of the concepts covered earlier. In this figure, two different stochastic optimization methods (described later in Sec. 4.7.2) are used for minimizing the generalized Griewank function over a 30 dimensional search space. The curves clearly show the exploration and exploitation phases for each of the methods: The fitness value drops rapidly during the exploration phase, followed by a much slower decay during the exploitation phase. As is evident, the method with the longer exploration phase finds a better fitness value. Note that in both cases, the methods do not converge to the true global minimum, which has a value of zero. The leveling off of the curves indicates that, due to the finite length of the exploration phase and consequent failure to maintain the convergence condition, convergence may not occur even if the number of iterations increases without limit.

In addition to the $\overline{f}^{(av)}$ plot, another common approach to comparing the performance of two methods is to perform a two-sample hypotheses test, such as Student's t-test or the Kolmogorov-Smirnov test [31], on the sample of final fitness values from multiple independent runs.

2.6 TUNING

While benchmarking is essential in the study and objective comparison of stochastic optimization methods, it does not guarantee, thanks to the NFL theorem, that the best performer on benchmark fitness functions will also work well in the intended application area. At best, benchmarking establishes the order in which one should investigate the effectiveness of a set of methods. Having arrived at an adequately performing method, one must undertake further statistical characterization in order to understand and improve its performance on the problem of interest. We call this process, which is carried out with the fitness functions pertaining to the actual application area, *tuning*.

To summarize, benchmarking is used for comparing optimization methods or delimiting the class of fitness functions that a method is good for. It is carried out with fitness functions that are crafted to be computationally cheap but sufficiently challenging. Tuning is the process of improving the performance of a method on the actual problem of interest and involves computing the actual fitness function (or surrogates).

A pitfall in tuning is *over-tuning* the performance of an optimization method on one specific fitness function. This is especially important for statistical regression problems because the fitness function, such as the least squares function in Eq. 1.4, depends on the data realization and, hence, changes every time the data realization changes. Thus, over-tuning the performance for a particular data realization runs the danger of worsening the performance of the method on other real-

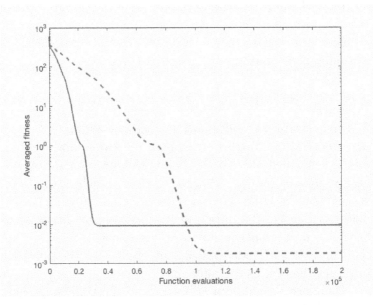

Figure 2.2 Fitness value averaged over independent trials for two different stochastic optimization methods. The X-axis shows the number of fitness evaluations. The fitness function is the 30-dimensional generalized Griewank function (Eq. 2.6) with each dimension of the search space confined to the interval $[-600, 600]$. For each curve, the averaging was performed over 30 independent runs. The two methods have different durations for the exploration phase, which extends out to roughly 3×10^4 and 1×10^5 function evaluations for the solid and dashed curves respectively. Details of the methods used are provided in Sec. 4.7.2.

izations. In fact, this situation is pretty much guaranteed to occur due to the NFL theorem.

Tuning of optimization methods for statistical regression problems must be carried out using metrics that are based on a sufficiently large set of data realizations. This almost always requires using *simulated data* since there may just be one realization of real data that is available. The use of simulations in tuning is covered in more detail in Ch. 5.

2.7 BMR STRATEGY

A simple strategy to safeguard against over-tuning is *best-of-M-runs* (BMR). In this strategy, a stochastic optimization method is tuned only to the point where a moderate probability, p_{hit}, of success in any single run is achieved. (Here, success is to be interpreted in the sense of landing in an optimality region but it can be redefined, as will be discussed in Sec 5.2.1, for parametric statistical regression problems.) One then performs M independent runs and picks the one that produces the best fitness value.

There are several notable features of the BMR approach. One is that the probability of failure across all the runs decreases exponentially as $(1 - p_{hit})^M$. Equivalently, the probability of success in at least one run increases rapidly with M. For example, if $p_{hit} = 0.5$, the probability of failure in $M = 10$ runs is only $\approx 10^{-3}$. In other words, success in finding the global minimum is practically assured.

The second feature is that the effort needed to tune a stochastic optimization method to perform moderately well is often significantly smaller than getting it to perform very well. This is especially true as the dimensionality of the search space increases. Hence, the BMR approach reduces the burden on the user in terms of tuning.

The third feature of BMR is that it falls in the class of so-called *embarrassingly parallel problems* that are the easiest to implement in a parallel computing environment. This is because each run can be executed by a parallel worker completely independently of the other runs, and does not involve the often tricky part of managing communications between processes in a parallel program. Since different runs occupy different processors, the execution time of the BMR strategy is essentially independent of M. Thus, it is as computationally cheap as a single run provided one has access to a sufficient number of processors.

Another factor in favor of BMR is that, having reached a plateau in Moore's law for the packing density of transistors on a chip, the chip industry is moving towards more processing cores to sustain future growth in computing power. This will drive down the dollar cost of the BMR strategy for optimization applications even further.

Finally, since the stochastic optimization method is only moderately tuned for any one run, the BMR strategy prevents overtuning on any particular fitness function.

2.8 PSEUDO-RANDOM NUMBERS AND STOCHASTIC OPTIMIZATION

An issue of practical importance when using stochastic optimization methods is that of random number generation. On computers, random numbers are generated using deterministic algorithms. In this sense, they are *pseudo-random* numbers that are not the trial values of a true random variable. However, if one does not know which algorithm is generating these numbers and its initial state, they satisfy the criteria of unpredictability of the next trial value based on past values. Once the initial state of the algorithm is specified, by specifying an integer called a *seed*, the sequence of numbers produced by it is predictable and reproducible.

All PRNGs have a *cycle length* (or period) for the sequences they produce. This is the number of trial values one can produce using a given seed before the sequence starts to repeat. In practice, most of the standard PRNGs have very long periods and one does not worry about exceeding them in typical applications. However, stochastic optimization methods are random number hungry algorithms and more so if coupled with the BMR strategy. Moreover, a long cycle length does not mean that the quality of the random number stream remains the same throughout. Therefore, it is best to err on the side of conserving the number of draws from a PRNG in stochastic optimization. In the context of BMR, this can be done by fixing the seeds for the PRNGs used by the independent parallel runs. While the fitness function may change, and itself may be a major consumer of PRNGs in the case of statistical regression applications, this ensures that the BMR consumes only a limited number of random numbers.

The reproducibility of a PRNG actually has some advantages when it comes to stochastic optimization. Fixing the seed allows the entire search sequence of a stochastic optimization method on a given fitness function to be reproduced exactly. This is usually invaluable in understanding its behavior in response to changes in its parameters or changes in the fitness function. Thus, the reader is encouraged to look carefully at the use of PRNGs when benchmarking or tuning a given method.

2.9 NOTES

The mathematically rigorous approach to optimization theory is well described in [46]. A comprehensive list of fitness functions commonly used in the benchmarking of stochastic optimization methods is provided in Table I of [4]. Deterministic optimization methods are described in great detail in [34]. The curse of dimensionality is discussed in the context of statistical analysis and machine learning in Ch. 2 of [16] and Ch. 5 of [19] respectively. Exploration and exploitation have been encountered in many different optimization scenarios. A good review can be found in [5]. The methodology for comparative assessment of optimization algorithms (i.e., benchmarking) is discussed critically in [2], which also includes references for the BMR strategy. For an insightful study of PRNGs, the reader may consult the classic text [29] by Knuth.

CHAPTER 3

Evolutionary Computation and Swarm Intelligence

CONTENTS

An overview is provided of stochastic optimization methods with a focus on the ones, generically called *evolutionary computation* (EC) or SI algorithms, that are derived from models of biological systems. The main goal of this chapter is to ease the novice user of EC and SI methods into this dauntingly diverse field by providing some guideposts.

3.1 OVERVIEW

The universe of stochastic optimization methods is vast and continues to inflate all the time. However, it is possible to discern some well-established approaches in the literature, called *metaheuristics*, that most stochastic optimization methods can be grouped under. This classification is only useful as an organizing principle that helps in comprehending the diversity of methods. There is a continuous flow of ideas between the metaheuristics and the boundaries are not at all impermeable. In fact, there is no universal agreement on the list of metaheuristics themselves. Therefore, our partial list of metaheuristics below should by no means be seen as either exhaustive or definitive.

- **Random sampling**: Methods in this group treat the fitness function as a joint pdf over the search space (normalization of the pdf is unnecessary) and draw trial values from it. The frequency with which any region of the search space hosts a trial outcome then depends on the fitness value in that region, allowing the global maximizer to be identified as the point around which the frequency of trial outcomes is the highest. (Recall that any minimization problem is equivalent to a maximization problem and vice versa.) The random sampling metaheuristic is derived from the theory of *Markov chains* [41], a class of memory-less stochastic processes.

- **Randomized local optimization**: The main idea here is to inject some randomness in the way deterministic optimization methods, such as steepest descent, work so that they can extricate themselves from local minima. The *stochastic gradient descent* method, which is used widely in the training of neural networks in machine learning, is an example under this metaheuristic.

- **Nature-inspired optimization**:

  - **Physics based**: *Simulated Annealing* [28] is a well-known method that is based on a model of how a molten metal turns into a crystal as its temperature is reduced. As it cools, the system of atoms searches stochastically through different possible spatial configurations, which correspond to different internal energies, until the crystalline configuration with the lowest energy is found.

This process is mimicked in simulated annealing by treating points in the search space as different configurations of a system and the fitness function as the energy associated with each configuration. A random walk is performed in the space, with the probability of transitioning to a point with a worse fitness than the current point decreasing as the iteration progresses. The change in the transition probability is controlled by a parameter called the temperature that is decreased following some user-specified schedule.

- **Biology based**: The hallmark of the methods in this class is the use of a population of *agents* in the search space with some means of communication between them. An agent is nothing but a location in the search space at which the fitness function is evaluated. However, the agents and their means of communication are modeled in a rudimentary way after actual biological organisms and systems. Within biology based optimization methods, one can further distinguish two metaheuristics, namely EC and SI that are discussed in more detail below.

3.2 EVOLUTIONARY COMPUTATION

Biological evolution of species is nothing but an optimization algorithm that moves the genetic makeup of a population of organisms towards higher fitness in their environment. The elementary picture of evolution, which is more than sufficient for our purpose, is that individuals in a species have variations in their genetic code that is brought about by mutation and gene mixing through sexual reproduction. Over multiple generations, the process of natural selection operates on the population to weed out individuals with genetic traits that result in lower fitness. Individuals with higher fitness in any given generation have a better chance at surviving and go on to produce offsprings that share the beneficial genetic trait. This results in the advantageous genetic trait gradually spreading throughout the population.

The idea of evolution as an optimization algorithm forms the foundation of the EC metaheuristic. A method under this metaheuristic is also known as a *Genetic Algorithm* (GA). The origin of GA methods dates back to early attempts at modeling biological evolution on computers.

A typical GA is an iterative algorithm that has the following components. (An iteration is more commonly called a *generation* in the GA literature.)

- A population of *genomes*, where a genome is simply a representation of a point in the search space. GAs were initially designed to handle discrete optimization problems. For such problems, one of the commonly used genomic representations encodes the possible integer values of each coordinate as a binary string with a specified number of bits.

- The fitness of a genome, which is simply the value of the fitness function at the location encoded in the genome.

- A *Crossover operation* that takes two or more genomes, called *parents*, as input and produces one or more new genomes, called *children*, as an output.

- A *Mutation operation* that creates random changes in a genome.

- A *Selection operation* that picks the members of the current generation (parents and children) who will survive to the next generation. Following natural evolution, the fitness of a genome only governs the probability of its survival. The number of genomes left after selection is kept constant in each generation.

The normal sequence in which the above operations are applied in any one generation is: Crossover → Mutation → Selection. The initialization of the iterations consists of picking the locations of the genomes randomly, such as by drawing a trial value for each bit with equal probabilities for getting 0 or 1. A variety of termination conditions have been proposed in the GA literature, the simplest being the production of a user-specified number of generations.

The limitation imposed by a binary genomic representation for optimization in continuous search spaces is overcome in a GA called *differential evolution* (DE) [45]. In DE, the genomic representation of a location in the search space is simply its position vector. For each parent, the crossover and mutation operations involve mixing its genes with those obtained by linearly combining three other randomly picked individuals. The selection operation picks the parent or the child based on their fitness values.

3.3 SWARM INTELLIGENCE

SI methods are based on modeling the cooperative behavior often seen in groups (swarms) or societies of biological organisms. The main difference between the SI and EC metaheuristics is that agents in SI are not born and do not die from one generation to the next. Agents in an SI method also move around in the search space like in EC methods, but the rules governing the change in location are modeled after how organisms in a collective communicate. SI methods are the newest entrants in the field of biology inspired optimization methods and have proven to be competitive with EC methods in most application areas.

The reasons behind the tendency of certain organisms, such as birds, fish and insects, to form collectives are quite varied but generally center around the search for food and avoiding predators. The behavior of swarms, such as a flock of birds or a school of fish, can be quite complex as a whole but the rules governing the behavior of individuals in a swarm are likely quite simple. This is simply a byproduct of the fact that an individual inside a dense swarm has limited visibility of what the rest of the swarm is doing. It can only process the detailed behavior of just a few individuals in its neighborhood while inferring some sort of an average for the behavior of more distant individuals. Numerical simulations of swarms support this hypothesis regarding local rules of behavior.

The same principle operates in large animal or insect societies. In an ant colony, for instance, a single ant is not capable of making sophisticated decisions on its own. However, through simple rules governing the behavior of each ant, the ant society as a whole is able to construct remarkably sophisticated structures, find large enough food caches to support itself, and mount effective defenses against much larger predators. Unlike swarms such as bird flocks that rely mostly on vision, individual ants react to chemical signaling that has contributions from not just its nearest neighbors but potentially the entire colony. This is reflected in models of the foraging behavior of ants, where each ant not only follows the chemical tracers left behind by other ants but also adds to the tracer to increase its concentration.

Both types of collective behaviors seen in swarms and colonies are modeled in SI methods. The prime example of the former type is *particle swarm optimization* (PSO), which will be the focus of the next chapter and the remainder of the book. The main example of the latter is *Ant Colony Optimization* (ACO). While PSO is better suited to optimization problems in continuous search spaces, ACO is aimed at discrete optimization.

3.4 NOTES

Methods under the random sampling metaheuristic are popular in Bayesian statistical analysis and a good description of the latter can be found in [18, 38]. Randomized local optimization methods play a key role in the training of artificial neural networks: See [19]. A comprehensive review of EC and SI algorithms, along with references to the original papers, is provided in [14]. The journal *IEEE Transactions on Evolutionary Computation* provides an excellent portal into the literature on EC and SI methods. Many of the seminal works in both fields have been reported in this journal. The biological models behind EC and SI algorithms are discussed in [12].

A promising new physics-based approach, called *quantum annealing*, is emerging on the horizon that has the potential to revolutionize how optimization problems are solved [3]. This approach is based on programming an optimization problem onto a new type of computing hardware [22], called a quantum annealer, that exploits the laws of quantum mechanics. While major corporations are already working on testing this approach, it remains to be seen whether and when it becomes mainstream.

Particle Swarm Optimization

CONTENTS

This chapter contains detailed descriptions of some of the principal variants under the PSO metaheuristic. The emphasis in this chapter is on getting the reader up-and-running with a successful implementation of PSO rather than providing a deep theoretical analysis. As such, the chapter contains some practical advice that can help the beginner in writing a correct and efficient PSO code.

In common with all EC and SI algorithms (see Ch. 3), the PSO metaheuristic consists of a population (*swarm*) of agents (*particles*) that move iteratively in the search space of an optimization problem. (Throughout this chapter, the search space will be assumed to be a D-dimensional hypercube.) The movement of each particle is determined by a vector, called its *velocity*[1], that provides its future location. The heart of any PSO algorithm is in the rules, called the *dynamical equations*, that govern the velocity update from one iteration to the next. Variants of PSO differ mostly in terms of the dynamical equations that they use.

4.1 KINEMATICS: GLOBAL-BEST PSO

The essence of the velocity update rules in global-best PSO is that a particle explores the search space randomly but constantly feels an attractive force towards the best location, in terms of fitness function value, it has found so far and the best location found by the swarm so far. These two locations are respectively called the particle-best (*pbest*) and global-best (*gbest*). As such, global-best PSO is also commonly called *gbest PSO*.

The mathematical notation for the quantities defined above, which establish the kinematics of the gbest PSO algorithm, are summarized in Table 4.1. The same quantities are shown pictorially in Fig. 4.1. As we will see later, these kinematical quantities remain essentially the same across the different variants of PSO but may be substituted with alternatives in some cases. Let $f(\overline{x})$ denote the fitness function that is being minimized. Then,

$$f\left(\overline{p}^{(i)}[k]\right) = \min_{j \leq k} f\left(\overline{x}^{(i)}[j]\right) , \qquad (4.1)$$

$$f\left(\overline{g}[k]\right) = \min_{j} f\left(\overline{p}^{(j)}[k]\right) , \qquad (4.2)$$

define pbest and gbest.

---

[1]If we adhere strictly to physics terminology, a more appropriate name would be the displacement vector.

Symbol	Description
N_{part}	The number of particles in the swarm.
$\overline{x}^{(i)}[k]$	Position of the ith particle at the kth iteration.
$\overline{v}^{(i)}[k]$	Velocity of the ith particle at the kth iteration.
$\overline{p}^{(i)}[k]$	Best location found by the ith particle (pbest).
$\overline{g}[k]$	Best location found by the swarm (gbest).

Table 4.1 Symbols used for describing kinematical quantities in the gbest PSO algorithm.

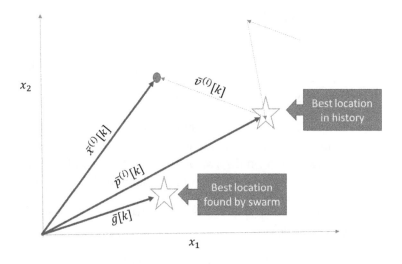

Figure 4.1 Kinematical quantities in the gbest PSO algorithm illustrated for a 2-dimensional search space. The dotted line shows the trajectory of the a particle over a few iterations before the current (k^{th}) one.

4.2   DYNAMICS: GLOBAL-BEST PSO

The dynamical rules for updating the velocity of particles in gbest PSO are given below.
Velocity update:

$$
\overline{v}^{(i)}[k+1] = w\overline{v}^{(i)}[k] + \mathbf{R}_1 c_1 \overline{F}_c^{(i)}[k] + \mathbf{R}_2 c_2 \overline{F}_s^{(i)}[k], (4.3)
$$

$$
\overline{F}_c^{(i)}[k] = \overline{p}^{(i)}[k] - \overline{x}^{(i)}[k] , \tag{4.4}
$$

$$
\overline{F}_s^{(i)}[k] = \overline{g}[k] - \overline{x}^{(i)}[k] . \tag{4.5}
$$

Velocity clamping: For each component $v_j^{(i)}[k+1]$, $j = 0, 1, \ldots, D-1$, of $\overline{v}^{(i)}[k+1]$,

$$
v_j^{(i)}[k+1] = \begin{cases} v_{\max} & \text{if } v_j^{(i)}[k+1] > v_{\max} \\ -v_{\max} & \text{if } v_j^{(i)}[k+1] < -v_{\max} \end{cases} , (4.6)
$$

where $v_{\max}$ is a positive number.
Position update:

$$
\overline{x}^{(i)}[k+1] = \overline{x}^{(i)}[k] + \overline{v}^{(i)}[k+1] . \tag{4.7}
$$

In the velocity update equation:

- $\mathbf{R}_i$, $i = 1, 2$, is a diagonal matrix with each diagonal element being an independently drawn trial value, at each iteration, of a random variable R having a uniform pdf, $p_R(x) = 1$ for $x \in [0, 1]$ and zero outside this interval.

- The parameter $w \in \mathbb{R}^+$ is a positive number called the *inertia weight*.

- $c_i \in \mathbb{R}^+$, $i = 1, 2$, is called an *acceleration constant*.

- $\overline{F}_c^{(i)}[k]$ is a vector pointing from the current location of the particle towards its current pbest.

- $\overline{F}_s^{(i)}[k]$ is a vector pointing from the current location of the particle towards the current gbest.

4.2.1 Initialization and termination

To complete the description of the algorithm, we need to specify its initialization and termination conditions.

Initialization in gbest PSO is fairly straightforward: (i) Each initial position, $\bar{x}^{(i)}[0]$, $0 \leq i \leq N_{\text{part}} - 1$, is assigned an independently drawn trial value from a joint uniform pdf over the search space. This simply means that each component $x_j^{(i)}[0]$, $0 \leq j \leq D-1$, is assigned an independently drawn trial value from the uniform pdf $U(x; a_j, b_j)$ (see App. A), with a_j and b_j being the minimum and maximum values along the jth dimension of the search space. (ii) Each initial velocity vector $\bar{v}^{(i)}[0]$ is first drawn independently from a joint uniform pdf, but one that is centered on $x^{(i)}[0]$ and confined to lie within the search space boundary. That is, each component $\bar{v}_j^{(i)}[0]$, $0 \leq j \leq D - 1$, is assigned an independently drawn trial value from the uniform pdf $U(x; a_j - x_j^{(i)}, b_j - x_j^{(i)})$. The initial velocity is then subjected to velocity clamping before starting the subsequent iterations.

The simplest termination condition is to stop the algorithm once a maximum number of iterations, N_{iter}, is reached. However, a number of more sophisticated termination conditions have been proposed in the literature. Some of these are enumerated in Sec. 4.7.

With the initialization, termination and dynamical equations defined, we can present an outline of the whole algorithm. This is displayed in Fig 4.2.

4.2.2 Interpreting the velocity update rule

The velocity update equation is quite straightforward to understand if one focuses on each of its terms in isolation. The *inertia term* $w\bar{v}^{(i)}[k]$ alone makes the next velocity vector point in the same direction as the current velocity. Hence, if this were the only term, a particle would simply move along a straight line. This makes the name of this term quite appropriate because the role of the inertia of a real object is indeed

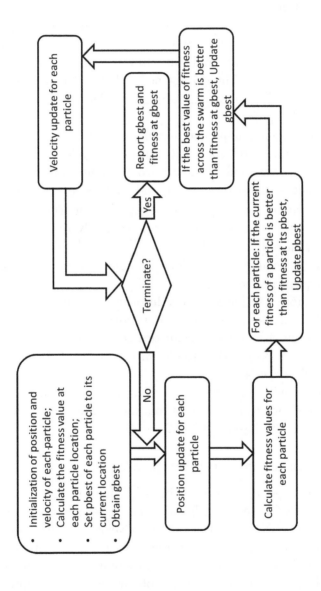

Figure 4.2 Schematic illustrating the PSO algorithm.

to maintain its state of motion and offer resistance to external forces that seek to change it.

The next term in the equation is called the *cognitive* term. If one considers $\overline{F}_c^{(i)}[k]$ alone, it is a force vector that wants to pull the particle towards pbest. The role of $\mathbf{R}_1$ in this term is to randomize this pull such that it is not always exactly attracting the particle towards pbest. In the same way, if one considers $\overline{F}_s^{(i)}[k]$ alone in the last term, which is called the *social* term, its role is to attract the particle towards gbest. Again the presence of $\mathbf{R}_2$ randomizes this pull so that it does not always point towards gbest. For each of the forces, the corresponding acceleration constant determines the importance (on average) of that force in the motion of a particle. Fig. 4.3 shows a cartoon to illustrate the meaning of cognitive and social forces using an analogy with a swarm of birds.

4.2.3 Importance of limiting particle velocity

During the course of their movement, some particles can acquire a velocity vector that, combined with their current location, can take them out of the boundary of the search space. In the early versions of PSO, it was found that for some settings of the algorithm parameters, most particles would leave the search space – a phenomenon called *particle explosion*. The occurrence of instabilities in iterative equations (e.g., $x[k + 1] = 5x[k]$ leads to an exponential increase in x) is well known and it is not surprising that something similar can happen in PSO.

In the early versions of PSO, particle explosion was tackled by velocity clamping as shown in Eq. 4.6. This was subsequently replaced by the inertia term with a weight $w < 1$. (An iterative equation of the form $x[k + 1] = wx[k]$ is then guaranteed to converge since the value of x keeps decreasing.) Present day versions of PSO use both velocity clamping and the inertia term but with a very generous clamping.

Another approach to limiting particle explosion is called *velocity constriction*, where the velocity update equation is

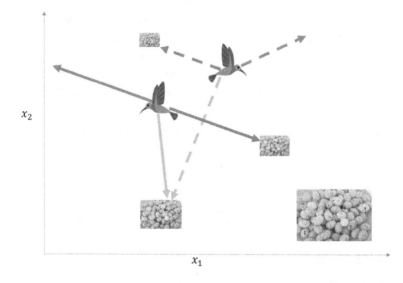

Figure 4.3 A cartoon that illustrates the nature of the inertia (red), cognitive (green) and social (yellow) terms. A bird swarm is searching for the best food source (i.e., best fitness value). The size of the picture of the food indicates how good it is. Each bird remembers the best food location it found in its own searching and has some desire to return back to it (cognitive term). At the same time it knows that the rest of the swarm has found a better food source and would like to move towards it (social term). All the while each bird also knows that there may be an even better food source that no member of the swarm has found. Hence, each one wants to continue searching (inertia term) and not be attracted completely towards either of the food sources found so far. Not shown here is the randomization of the cognitive and social forces, which is the key ingredient that makes PSO work.

altered as follows.

Velocity constriction:

$$\bar{v}^{(i)}[k+1] \;=\; K\left(\bar{v}_i[k] + \mathbf{R}_1 c_1 \overline{F}_c^{(i)} + \mathbf{R}_2 c_2 \overline{F}_s^{(i)}\right) . \;(4.8)$$

The factor K, called the *constriction factor*, is prescribed to be [11]

$$K \;=\; \frac{2}{\left|2 - \phi - \sqrt{\phi^2 - 4\phi}\right|} , \tag{4.9}$$

$$\phi \;=\; c_1 + c_2 > 4 . \tag{4.10}$$

Note that the velocity constriction expression on the RHS of Eq. 4.8 is the same as Eq. 4.3 if the inertia weight is pulled out as a common factor. Even when velocity constriction is not used, the acceleration constants c_1 and c_2 are, in most cases, set to $c_1 = c_2 = 2$ (or just around this value) in keeping with Eq. 4.10 above.

Whether one uses clamping or constriction, it is important to somehow limit the velocities of particles in order to keep them in the search space for a sufficiently large number of iterations.

4.2.4   Importance of proper randomization

The stochastic nature of the PSO algorithm arises from the random matrices $\mathbf{R}_1$ and $\mathbf{R}_2$ in Eq. 4.3. The most common mistake observed by the author in implementations of PSO by beginners is an improper use of randomization: It is very tempting for beginners to replace these matrices by scalar random variables. After all, it looks very natural that the particle experiences attractive forces that point towards pbest and gbest, which would be the case for scalar weights multiplying the vectors $\overline{F}_c^{(i)}$ and $\overline{F}_s^{(i)}$, but that have random strengths. However, this is a serious error!

Consider a particle at some iteration step k in a $D = 3$ dimensional search space for which $\bar{v}^{(i)}[k] = 0$. Then, if R_1 and R_2 are scalars, the velocity vector will be updated to some random vector lying in the plane formed by $\overline{F}_c^{(i)}$ and $\overline{F}_s^{(i)}$. If $\overline{F}_s^{(i)}$ does not change in the next update, the particle position as well as the new $\overline{F}_{c,s}^{(i)}$ vectors will continue to lie in the same plane. Hence, the next updated velocity vector will continue to lie in this plane, and so on. In fact, as long as $\overline{F}_s^{(i)}$ stays the same, all future velocity vectors will only cause the particle to move in the initial plane. (When $D > 3$ and the starting velocity is not zero, the motion will be confined to a 3-dimensional subspace of the D-dimensional space.)

This confinement to a restricted region of the full search space leads to inefficient exploration and, hence, loss of performance. On the other hand, if one uses the matrices $\mathbf{R}_1$ and $\mathbf{R}_2$, the particle moves off the initial plane even when the starting velocity vector is zero. Fig. 4.4 illustrates the difference between using scalar and matrix random variables, clearly showing that proper randomization is the most important ingredient of the velocity update equation.

4.2.5 Role of inertia

The role of the inertia term is to prevent the particle from being attracted too strongly by the cognitive and social forces. In this way, it encourages exploration in the algorithm. The inertia weight w is usually kept between 0 and 1 since higher values can quickly lead to runaway growth in the velocity, thereby forcing it to stay at the clamped value throughout most of the iterations.

Keeping the inertia weight at a value close to unity promotes exploration but also prevents the particles from responding to the attractive forces. This keeps them from entering the exploitation phase in which they should start converging towards a promising region of the search space that is likely to contain the global minimum. Hence, the standard prescription is to allow the inertia weight to start out near unity and decay to a small value as the iterations progress. Typically, one starts with $w = 0.9$ and allows it to decay linearly to a more moderate value, such as 0.4, as the algorithm

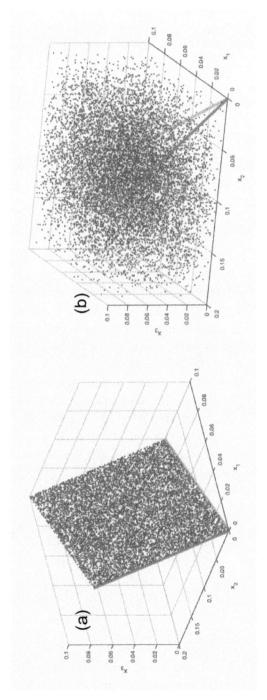

Figure 4.4 A large number of trial outcomes from the probability distribution of $\bar{v}^{(i)}[k+1]$ when $\bar{v}^{(i)}[k] = (0,0,0)$ and the random factors multiplying the social and cognitive forces in the velocity update equation are (a) scalars (i.e., same for all the velocity components), and (b) matrices (i.e., different random numbers for different velocity components). The search space in this illustration is 3-dimensional. The particle position $\bar{x}^{(i)}[k]$ is the origin and the red (green) line points from the origin to the pbest (gbest). (For this illustration, we set $w = 0.9$, $c_1 = c_2 = 1.0$.)

approaches termination. Thus, the inertia weight is given by

$$w[k] = -\frac{0.5}{N_{\text{iter}} - 1}(k - 1) + 0.9 , \qquad (4.11)$$

for termination based on a maximum number of iterations.

4.2.6 Boundary condition

It is quite possible that the velocity update equation generates a velocity vector that, despite clamping, moves a particle out of the search space. An important part of the PSO algorithm is the specification of the *boundary conditions* to use when this happens.

A number of boundary conditions have been explored in the literature. However, it has often been found that the so-called *let them fly* boundary condition tends to work best. Under this condition, no change is made to the dynamical equations if a particle exits the search space. The only thing that happens is that its fitness value is set to $+\infty$ if the problem is that of minimization (or $-\infty$ if maximizing). Since the particle has the worst possible fitness value outside the search space, its pbest does not change and, consequently, neither is the gbest affected. Eventually, the attractive forces from these two locations, which are always within the search space, pull the particle back. At this point, it rejoins the swarm and searches the space in the normal way.

Other boundary conditions that have been proposed include the so-called *reflecting walls* and *absorbing walls* conditions. These require overriding the velocity update equation when a boundary crossing is detected for a particle. In the former case, the sign of the component of velocity perpendicular to the boundary being breached is flipped. In the latter, this component is set to zero.

4.3 KINEMATICS: LOCAL-BEST PSO

The local-best variant of PSO, also called *lbest PSO*, involves a single change to the dynamical equations of gbest PSO. This one change has been observed across a large range of statistical regression problems to make lbest PSO much more effective at locating the global optimum. However, we remind the reader that, following the NFL theorem (see Sec. 2.3), there will always exist optimization problems where lbest PSO performs worse than other variants.

For lbest PSO, we first need to define the concept of a particle *neighborhood*. The neighborhood $\mathbb{N}^{(i)}$ of the ith particle is simply a subset, including i, of the set of indices labeling the particles in the swarm.

$$\mathbb{N}^{(i)} \;=\; \mathbb{I}^{(i)} \cup \{i\}\,, \tag{4.12}$$

$$\mathbb{I}^{(i)} \;\subseteq\; \{1, 2, \ldots, N_{\text{part}}\} \setminus \{i\}\,. \tag{4.13}$$

($\mathbb{A} \setminus \mathbb{B}$, called the *absolute complement* of $\mathbb{B} \subset \mathbb{A}$ in $\mathbb{A}$, is the set of elements in $\mathbb{A}$ that are not in $\mathbb{B}$.) The number of elements in $\mathbb{N}^{(i)}$ is called *neighborhood size* for the ith particle.

For a given particle and iteration k, the local-best particle is the particle in its neighborhood whose pbest has the best fitness value. The location of the local-best particle, denoted by $\overline{l}^{(i)}[k]$, is called the *lbest* for the ith particle.

$$f(\overline{l}^{(i)}[k]) \;=\; \min_{j \in \mathbb{N}^{(i)}} f(\overline{p}^{(j)}[k])\,. \tag{4.14}$$

The definition of lbest is a generalization of gbest. The gbest location is simply the lbest when the neighborhood of each particle consists of all the particles in the swarm.

A particular specification of $\mathbb{N}^{(i)}$ for each i is said to define a particular *topology*. The topology described above, where each particle has the same lbest (i.e., the gbest), is called the *gbest topology*. A less trivial topology is the so-called *ring topology*. Here, each particle has the same neighborhood size, given by $2m + 1$ for some specified m, and

$$\mathbb{N}^{(i)} \;=\; \{r(i - k); -m \le k \le m,\, m \ge 1\}\,, \tag{4.15}$$

$$r(j) \;=\; \begin{cases} j & 1 \le j \le N_{\text{part}}\,, \\ j + N_{\text{part}} & j < 1\,, \\ j - N_{\text{part}} & j > N_{\text{part}} \end{cases} \tag{4.16}$$

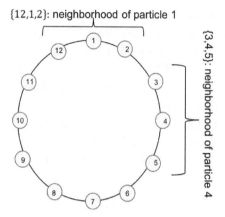

Figure 4.5 Graph representation of the ring topology with a neighborhood size of 3 for a swarm consisting of 12 particles. Each node in this graph indicates a particle and an edge connecting two nodes indicates that they belong to the same neighborhood. Note that every particle in this topology belongs to three different neighborhoods (one of which is its own).

Fig. 4.5 illustrates the the ring topology using a graph.

4.4 DYNAMICS: LOCAL-BEST PSO

The dynamical rules for lbest PSO remain the same as those of gbest PSO except for the change $\overline{F}_s^{(i)}[k] \rightarrow \overline{l}^{(i)}[k] - \overline{x}^{(i)}[k]$. (The initialization and termination conditions for lbest PSO are the same as those in Sec. 4.2.1.)

Velocity update (lbest PSO):

$$\overline{v}^{(i)}[k+1] = w\overline{v}^{(i)}[k] + \mathbf{R}_1 c_1 \overline{F}_c^{(i)}[k] + \mathbf{R}_2 c_2 \overline{F}_s^{(i)}[k] \quad (4.17)$$

$$\overline{F}_c^{(i)}[k] = \overline{p}^{(i)}[k] - \overline{x}^{(i)}[k] , \quad (4.18)$$

$$\overline{F}_s^{(i)}[k] = \overline{l}^{(i)}[k] - \overline{x}^{(i)}[k] . \quad (4.19)$$

The main significance of replacing gbest with lbest is that any given particle is not immediately aware of the best fitness found by the whole swarm. It only knows about the best fitness in its own neighborhood at any given iteration step. However, since every particle is part of multiple neighborhoods (see Fig. 4.5), the information about gbest gradually percolates down to every particle. This happens at a much slower rate (in terms of iteration number) compared to gbest PSO. The end result is that particles spend more time in the exploration phase since they are not all attracted towards the same current best fitness location. For the same fitness function, this generally increases the number of iterations required for lbest PSO to converge to the global optimum, but the probability of convergence goes up significantly.

4.5 STANDARDIZED COORDINATES

Consider a search space $\mathbb{D} \subset \mathbb{R}^D$ that is in the form of a D-dimensional hypercube with each component x_i, $i = 0, 1, \ldots, D$, of the position vector $\overline{x} \in \mathbb{D}$ obeying $x_i \in [a_i, b_i]$, $b_i - a_i > 0$. One can reparametrize the search space by shifting to translated and normalized coordinates $s_i = (x_i - a_i)/(b_i - a_i)$ such that $s_i \in [0, 1]$. We call s_i a *standardized coordinate*.

Coordinate standardization is a great convenience when writing a code for PSO since the information about the actual interval $[a_i, b_i]$, and the inversion of s_i to the actual x_i, can be hidden in the code for the fitness function. Alternatively, the interval $[a_i, b_i]$ can be passed to the PSO code, which in turn simply passes it to the fitness function [2]. With standardization, the PSO code is written such that it always searches a D-dimensional hypercube with side lengths of unity irrespective of the actual size of the search hypercube.

Standardization only works if the search space is a hypercube. But this is actually a tacit assumption embedded in the design of PSO itself. In fact, the performance of PSO suffers

---

[2]Further simplification can be achieved by using a C-style pointer to the fitness function as an input argument, making the PSO code completely independent of the fitness function it is applied to.

if it runs in a search space with too complicated a shape. This mainly happens due to the leakage of an excessive number of particles from the search space, reducing the effectiveness of the exploration phase of the search.

4.6 RECOMMENDED SETTINGS FOR REGRESSION PROBLEMS

In the author's experience with regression problems, both gbest and lbest PSO perform well but the performance of the latter becomes better as the number of parameters increases. For non-parametric problems, which tend to have higher search space dimensionalities, lbest PSO is certainly the better option. The choice between the two often boils down to the computational cost of the methods. As mentioned above, lbest PSO generally takes more iterations to converge. This entails a larger number of fitness evaluations, which increases the overall computational cost of the method since the cost of fitness evaluation in regression problems always dominates over that of the PSO dynamical equations and bookkeeping.

Regarding the settings for the parameters in both gbest and lbest PSO, an in-depth study on benchmark fitness functions is reported in [4]. Based on [4] and our own experience, the recommended settings for non-linear regression problems involving more than ≈ 2 parameters (or almost any non-parametric regression problem) are summarized in Table 4.2.

4.7 NOTES

PSO was proposed by Kennedy and Eberhart in [27]. The important idea of an inertia weight was introduced in [43]. Velocity constriction was obtained from an analytical study of a simplified PSO in [8]. A text that goes deeper into the theoretical foundations of PSO is [7]. Performance under different boundary conditions is studied in [39].

Setting Name	Setting Value
Position initialization	$x_j^{(i)}[0]$ drawn from $U(x; 0, 1)$
Velocity initialization	$v_j^{(i)}[0]$ drawn from $U(x; 0, 1) - x_j^{(i)}[0]$
$v_{\max}$	0.5
N_{part}	40
$c_1 = c_2$	2.0
$w[k]$	Linear decay from 0.9 to 0.4
Boundary condition	Let them fly
Termination condition	Fixed number of iterations
lbest PSO	Ring topology; Neighborhood size = 3

Table 4.2 Recommended settings for gbest and lbest PSO in the case of regression problems. The search space coordinates are assumed to be standardized.

While we have cited some of the important original papers above, the PSO literature is too vast to be reviewed properly in this book. The reader interested in delving deeper into the PSO literature should consult books such as [14] or can easily find up to date reviews through web searches. We will now discuss some of the PSO variations that have been explored in the literature. Again, this is by no means intended to be a comprehensive review and we do not attempt to reference all the original papers.

4.7.1 Additional PSO variants

In this chapter, we have discussed two out of the many variants of PSO that have been proposed in the literature. The main reason for exploring variations in algorithms under any particular metaheuristic is that there is still no comprehensive theoretical understanding, if something like this is at all possible, of what makes these algorithms succeed in any given instance. In fact the NFL theorem promises us that every variant will have an associated set of optimization problems where it will be the best performer. That said, it is important to understand that creating a new variant should not be taken up lightly because our intuitive prediction of its behavior in a high-dimensional search space may be very far from its actual behavior.

One set of variations is in the termination condition. While termination based on a fixed number of iterations is the simplest, one does not have an intuitive way of fixing this parameter. Some alternatives are listed below.

- In some optimization problems, we know the minimum value $f_{\min}$ of the fitness function but we need the location of the minimum. In such problems, the natural termination criterion is to stop when $f(\overline{g}[k]) - f_{\min} \leq \epsilon$, where ϵ is a sufficiently small threshold set by the user.

- Stop at step $k_{\max}$ if the change in gbest averaged over some number, K, of past iterations is small: $(1/K) \sum_{i=0}^{K-1} \|\overline{g}[k_{\max} - i] - \overline{g}[k_{\max} - i - 1]\| < \epsilon$. Here, the user needs to fix K and ϵ.

- Stop at step $k_{\max}$ if the velocity averaged over some number, K, of past iterations and over the swarm is small: $(1/K) \sum_{j=0}^{K-1} \sum_{i=1}^{N_{\mathrm{part}}} \|\overline{v}^{(i)}[k_{\max} - j]\| < \epsilon$. Here, the user needs to fix K and ϵ.

- Stop at step $k_{\max}$ if the change in the fitness value averaged over some number, K, of past iterations is small:

$$\frac{1}{K} \sum_{i=0}^{K-1} \left(f\left(\overline{g}[k_{\max} - i]\right) - f\left(\overline{g}[k_{\max} - i - 1]\right) \right) < \epsilon \, .$$

- Define the *swarm radius*, $R[k] = \max_i \|\overline{x}^{(i)}[k] - \overline{g}[k]\|$ and the normalized swarm radius, $r[k] = R[k]/R[1]$. Stop at step $k_{\max}$ if the normalized swarm radius is small: $r[k_{\max}] \leq \epsilon$. Here, the user needs to fix ϵ.

Some alternatives to the linear inertia decay law are as follows.

- The inertia $w[k]$ is a random variable with a uniform pdf over some interval $[w_1, w_2]$ with $w_2 < 1.0$. This tends to lengthen the exploration phase of PSO.

- Non-linear decrease in inertia.

Several variations in the dynamical equations of PSO have been proposed. In one class of variations, called *memetic searches*, a local minimzation method (e.g., steepest descent) is incorporated into PSO [36]. For some fitness functions, memetic searches are more efficient since the local minimization can move the search more efficiently to the global minimum. However, memetic searches also tend to have a shortened exploration phase that can be detrimental for very rugged fitness functions.

An interesting variant of PSO is *Standard PSO* (SPSO) [53]. This is an algorithm that has gone through several versions and seeks to capture the latest advances in PSO research. The motivation behind SPSO is to present a baseline, well-characterized algorithm against which new variants can be compared. One of the key features of SPSO is that it changes the distribution of the velocity vector compared to the distribution seen in gbest or lbest PSO (see Fig. 4.4). For the latter two, the distribution is aligned along the coordinate axes of the search space. This can be disadvantageous if the fitness function is rotated while keeping the same coordinates since the distribution, which will remain aligned along the axes, will not be well-adapted to the rotated fitness function. In SPSO, the distribution becomes spherical in shape making it insensitive to a rotation of the fitness function.

4.7.2 Performance example

Previously, in Fig. 2.2, we showed the performance of two stochastic optimization methods on the generalized Griewank benchmark function. The two methods, corresponding to the solid and dashed curves in Fig. 2.2, are gbest and lbest PSO respectively. The parameters of both the methods were set to the prescribed values in Table 4.2 except for the linear decay of inertia. For gbest PSO, the inertia decayed from 0.9 to 0.4 over 500 iterations, while the same drop in inertia happened over 2000 iterations for lbest PSO. In both cases, the total number of iterations at termination was 5000 and the inertia remains constant over the remaining iterations once it reaches its lowest value.

PSO Applications

CONTENTS

This chapter describes the application of PSO to concrete parametric and non-parametric regression problems. Some common issues of practical importance in these problems are identified and possible ways to handle them are presented.

The regression problems that will be considered here are the examples described in Sec. 1.3.1 and Sec. 1.3.2 for parametric and non-parametric regression respectively.

5.1 GENERAL REMARKS

5.1.1 Fitness function

Statistical regression involves the optimization of a fitness function over a set of regression models. We have encountered two such fitness functions earlier, namely the likelihood and the least squares function. In the following, we will concentrate exclusively on the latter in which the optimization task is that of minimization.

In most regression problems, it is possible to organize the search for the global minimum of the fitness function as a set of nested minimizations. Consider the parametric regression example where we have 4 parameters defining the quadratic chirp: $\bar{\theta} = (A, a_1, a_2, a_3)$. Let θ' denote the subset (a_1, a_2, a_3). We can organize the minimization of the least squares function in Eq. 1.8 over these parameters as follows.

$$\min_{\bar{\theta}} L_S(\mathbb{T}; \bar{\theta}) = \min_{\bar{\theta}'} \left(\min_A L_S(\mathbb{T}; \bar{\theta}) \right), \tag{5.1}$$

$$= \min_{\bar{\theta}'} l_S(\bar{\theta}'), \tag{5.2}$$

$$l_S(\bar{\theta}') = \frac{1}{2\sigma^2} \min_A \sum_{i=0}^{N} (y_i - A\sin(\phi(x_i)))^2 . \tag{5.3}$$

It is straightforward to carry out the minimization in Eq. 5.3 analytically since one simply has a quadratic polynomial in A.

Similarly, the minimization of $L_S(\mathbb{T}; \bar{\theta})$ in the non-parametric regression example, where $\bar{\theta} = (\bar{\alpha}, \bar{b})$ (see Eq. 1.11), can be organized as an inner minimization over $\bar{\alpha}$ followed by an outer minimization over $\bar{b}$. Since $\bar{\alpha}$ appears linearly in the regression model, it can be minimized over analytically.

In the following, we will deal only with the function l_S that is left over after the inner minimizations in both the parametric and non-parametric examples. Therefore, l_S constitutes the fitness function for PSO and the minimization is over the set of parameters left over in the outer minimization step. The explicit forms of the function l_S for the parametric and non-parametric regression examples are derived in App. C.

In the general case, analytical minimizations should be carried out first before using a numerical minimization method if a regression model admits this possibility. Doing so significantly reduces the burden on the numerical method due to both (i) a reduction in the dimensionality of the search space, and (ii) a reduction in the ruggedness of the leftover fitness function.

5.1.2 Data simulation

In both the parametric and non-parametric examples, a data realization is of the form $\mathbb{T} = \{(y_i, x_i)\}$, $i = 0, 1, \ldots, N - 1$, where y_i is a trial value of $Y = f(X) + E$. In each data realization $y_i = f(x_i) + \epsilon_i$, $i = 0, 1, \ldots, N - 1$, where ϵ_i is a trial value of E, a normally distributed random variable with zero mean and unit variance.

For a data realization such as $\mathbb{T}$, let $\overline{x}$ denote $(x_0, x_1, \ldots, x_{N-1})$ and $\overline{y} = (y_0, y_1, \ldots, y_{N-1})$. It is convenient to refer to the sequence $(f(x_0), f(x_1), \ldots, f(x_{N-1}))$ present in a given $\overline{y}$ as the *signal*. The sequence $(\epsilon_0, \epsilon_1, \ldots, \epsilon_{N-1})$ in a data realization is called a *noise realization*. In both the examples, the elements of $\overline{x}$ are fixed and equally spaced: $x_i - x_{i-1}$, $i = 1, 2, \ldots, N - 1$, is constant. Thus, $\overline{x}$ stays the same in the different data realizations but $\overline{y}$ changes.

For the parametric example, we call the values of the parameters (A, a_1, a_2, a_3) that define the quadratic chirp present in the data as the *true signal parameters*. The quadratic chirp corresponding to the true signal parameters is called the *true signal*. While the true signal sequence used in the non-parametric example, $(f(x_0), f(x_1), \ldots, f(x_{N-1}))$, where $f(X) \propto B_{0,4}(X; \overline{b})$, is also defined by a set of parameters, we deliberately avoid references to its parameters because they are not directly estimated in non-parametric regression.

We will illustrate the application of PSO and measure its performance using multiple data realizations. Data realizations will be generated under both the null (H_0) and alternative (H_1) hypotheses (see Sec. 1.4). A data realization under H_0 consists of only a noise realization, while a realization under H_1 has a true signal added to a noise realization. In the H_1 data realizations, the true signal will be held fixed and only the noise realization will change from one realization to another. Since the noise realizations are obtained using a PRNG, the data realizations constitute *simulated* data.

As a measure of the overall strength of the signal in both the parametric and non-parametric examples, we use the *signal to noise ratio* (SNR) defined as,

$$\text{SNR} \; = \; \frac{1}{\sigma} \left[\sum_{i=0}^{N-1} f(x_i)^2 \right]^{\frac{1}{2}}, \qquad (5.4)$$

where σ^2 is the variance of the noise. Fixing the strength of a signal in terms of its SNR, instead of a parameter such as A in the case of the quadratic chirp, ensures that the effect of the signal on inferences drawn from the data is the same no matter the variance of the noise.

5.1.3 Parametric degeneracy and noise

Multiple local minima in statistical regression fitness functions arise from two sources. This is illustrated in Fig. 5.1 where the fitness function of the parametric regression example is shown across a 2-dimensional cross-section of the 3-dimensional search space.

We see that even when a data realization has no noise in it, the fitness function has multiple local minima. These local minima arise because the parameters used in the fitness function evaluation can conspire to make the associated quadratic chirp resemble the true signal. We call this source of local minima *parametric degeneracy* and it is a hallmark of non-linear regression models. When the data has noise in it, we see that additional local minima appear in the fitness function while the ones due to parametric degeneracy are shifted, suppressed, or enhanced.

A stochastic optimization method must escape these local minima while searching for the global minimum. While we

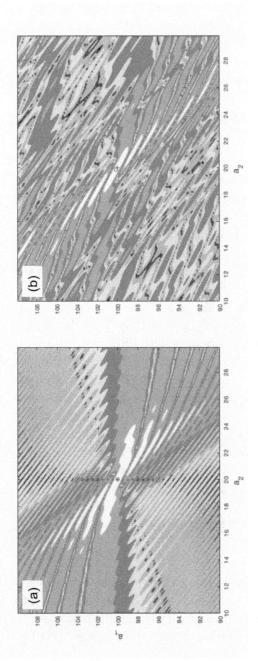

Figure 5.1 Contour plot of the fitness function for the quadratic chirp regression problem in Sec. 1.3.1. Shown here is a 2-dimensional cross-section of the 3-dimensional search space. In panel (a), the data, $\bar{y}$, is just a quadratic chirp, with $a_1 = 100$, $a_2 = 20$, $a_3 = 10$, without any added noise. In panel (b), there is noise present in $\bar{y}$ along with the quadratic chirp from (a). Areas with white color contain local minima. The location of the true parameters is marked by '+', while 'o' marks the global minimizer. The global minimizer coincides with the true parameters in (a) but not in (b). The fitness function is shown on a logarithmic scale because the local minima are not as prominent as the global minimum on a linear scale.

have no control over the noise induced local minima, every effort should be made to help the method by mitigating the ones due to parametric degeneracy. Not much can be done in the parametric regression example given here but this becomes a critical topic in non-parametric regression.

5.1.4 PSO variant and parameter settings

We use lbest PSO and the parameter settings listed in Table 4.2 for both the parametric and non-parametric regression examples. This illustrates a particularly advantageous feature of PSO in general compared to other stochastic optimization methods: its parameter settings need little tweaking, if at all, across a wide variety of problems. This remarkable robustness of the parameter settings is well-known in the PSO literature from empirical testing on benchmark functions but it also seems to carry over into the real-world regression problems that the author has dealt with.

From practical experience, the settings that do require tuning to achieve good performance with PSO are (i) the number of iterations, N_{iter}, for termination, and (ii) the number of independent PSO runs, N_{runs}, in the BMR strategy (see Sec. 2.7). The tuning of these parameters in the case of parametric regression can be performed using a fairly simple but effective strategy that will be described later. The tuning for non-parametric regression involves more of a seat-of-the-pants approach but it is greatly aided by the fact that there are only two such parameters that require tuning in most cases.

5.2 PARAMETRIC REGRESSION

5.2.1 Tuning

As discussed in Sec. 2.6, tuning of stochastic optimization methods in statistical regression problems should take into account a large number of data realizations. It is important to avoid the pitfall of over-tuning a method on a single or a few data realizations because, thanks to the NFL theorem, this is likely to result in a poor overall performance.

While a typical statistical regression problem involves just one data realization, one can always simulate multiple data realizations, as described in Sec. 5.1.2, for the purpose of tuning. These simulated data realizations need only be derived from a reasonably good approximation of the regression model for the tuning to work well on the actual data.

Since a regression problem that needs a stochastic optimization method is also often the one where a deterministic method is computationally infeasible, it is generally not possible to ascertain if the global minimum of the fitness function has been found successfully. Fortunately, in the case of parametric regression, there exists a surrogate condition that at least tells us if a stochastic optimization method is worth using or not. The same condition can also be used to set up a general purpose strategy for tuning the method.

Minimal performance condition: For a given simulated data realization, let f^{opt} be the fitness found by the stochastic optimization method and f^{true} be the fitness at the point in the search space corresponding to the true signal in the data. If the condition $f^{\mathrm{opt}} < f^{\mathrm{true}}$ is satisfied, the method can be said to have met the minimal performance expected of any statistical regression method.

The minimal performance condition is based on the fact that the global minimizer is always located away from the true values of the parameters when there is noise in the data. This is evident in the example shown in Fig. 5.1. Equivalently, $f^{\mathrm{opt}} < f^{\mathrm{true}}$. Hence, any stochastic optimization method should, at the very least, satisfy this condition even if we can never ascertain its success in finding the actual global minimum.

Ideally, the minimal performance condition should hold for any data realization for a well-performing stochastic optimization method. However, in practice, we can only ensure that this happens with a sufficiently high probability. The higher this probability, the lower is the effect of failure in localizing the global minimum on the statistical inference drawn from given data. This observation leads to the definition of a performance metric that can be used to tune any stochastic optimization method for parametric regression.

For concreteness, let us now focus on PSO where we need to tune only two parameters, namely N_{runs} and N_{iter}. Let $\mathcal{M}(N_{\mathrm{runs}}, N_{\mathrm{iter}})$ denote the performance metric. Then, for a set of N_{tune} data realizations, we define

$$\mathcal{M}(N_{\mathrm{runs}}, N_{\mathrm{iter}}) = \frac{N_{\mathrm{mpc}}}{N_{\mathrm{tune}}}, \qquad (5.5)$$

where N_{mpc} is the number of data realizations where the minimal performance condition was satisfied. In the next stage, one goes through different combinations of N_{runs} and N_{iter} until $\mathcal{M}(N_{\mathrm{runs}}, N_{\mathrm{iter}})$ reaches a sufficiently low value. This value depends on the requirements the user has on the quality of the solutions found by PSO as well as the available computational resources.

Fig. 5.2 illustrates the above process by taking two extreme combinations of N_{runs} and N_{iter}. Shown is the scatterplot of f^{opt} and f^{true} for $N_{\mathrm{tune}} = 100$ realizations of data. As expected for these extreme combinations, $\mathcal{M}(N_{\mathrm{runs}}, N_{\mathrm{iter}})$ goes from being nearly zero to being unity. For the parametric regression example, a reasonable setting for N_{runs} and N_{iter} lies somewhere in between these extremes.

Recalling that the tuning process only ensures a certain probability for success, obtaining $\mathcal{M}(N_{\mathrm{runs}}, N_{\mathrm{iter}}) = 1$ for the set of tuning data realizations does not mean that it will remain unity for a much larger number of realizations. Therefore, once a satisfactory setting for N_{runs} and N_{iter} has been found, it is always a good idea to validate the performance of the tuned PSO by running it on a much larger and independent set of *validation data* realizations. The validation should be done before analyzing the actual data with the tuned PSO.

Once PSO has been tuned using simulated data as described above and its performance validated to be acceptable, it can be applied to the actual data that needs to be ana-

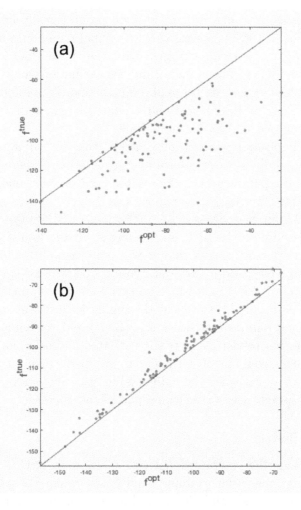

Figure 5.2 Scatterplot of f^{opt} and f^{true} for $N_{\mathrm{tune}} = 100$ realizations of data containing the quadratic chirp. The panels correspond to PSO with (a) $N_{\mathrm{runs}} = 2$, $N_{\mathrm{iter}} = 50$, and (b) $N_{\mathrm{runs}} = 8$, $N_{\mathrm{iter}} = 1000$. The minimal performance condition is satisfied when a point lies above the straight line representing $f^{\mathrm{opt}} = f^{\mathrm{true}}$. For (a), $\mathcal{M}(2, 50) = 0.07$, while $\mathcal{M}(8, 1000) = 1.0$ for (b). The same data realizations are used in both (a) and (b). The true signal parameters are $a_1 = 100$, $a_2 = 20$, $a_3 = 10$ and the SNR is 10.

lyzed. Since it would, in general, be computationally infeasible to check if PSO converged to the global minimum for the actual data, the result obtained with the tuned PSO is the best one can get. The more faithful the simulations are to the process that generated the real data, the more confident one can be that the PSO tuned and validated on simulated data has performed well for the actual data.

An important point to note here is that the tuning procedure described above is for a fixed true signal. This implies that all the parameters, including the SNR of the signal, are fixed across the N_{tune} data realizations. In general, this is not a major limitation because the performance of PSO typically depends only on the SNR and tuning it for the lowest SNR value of interest ensures that it will perform well for higher values as well. It does, however, require that we have an idea of how low in SNR we wish to go in a particular application. It does no harm also to repeat the tuning for different sets of true signal parameters (other than SNR) and verifying that the tuning is robust. A more sophisticated approach, not explored here, could involve using an overall performance metric that is an average over the individual metric values associated with a discrete set of true signal parameter values.

5.2.2 Results

Given that the computational cost of running PSO on the parametric regression example is quite low, we skip the metric-based tuning and validation step, leaving it as an exercise for the reader, and simply adopt the highest settings, $N_{runs} = 8$ and $N_{iter} = 1000$ (see Fig. 5.2). The results obtained with this setting and presented below serve as a reference for comparison when reproducing the performance of PSO on this example.

For each data realization, the minimizer found by PSO gives us the estimated values of the true signal parameters in that realization. Due to the presence of noise, the estimated value of a parameter is a random variable. Fig. 5.3 shows the marginal and pair-wise bivariate distributions of the estimated values of a_1, a_2, and a_3.

Fig. 5.3 also allows us to make a crude estimate of the computational cost of a grid-based search. A reasonable choice is to let the grid spacing along a given parameter be some fraction of the standard deviation of its estimated value. For a fractional spacing between 1 and 1/5 times the standard deviation, and using the search range and standard deviation of each parameter as shown in Fig. 5.3, we get the total number of grid points to be between $\approx 3.8 \times 10^5$ to $\approx 4.7 \times 10^7$ respectively. In contrast, the number of fitness evaluations in PSO is fixed at $40 \times 8 \times 1000 = 3.2 \times 10^5$, which is lower than the lowest estimate above for the grid-based search[1].

Fig. 5.4 shows the distribution of the GLRT (Eq. 1.17) under H_0 and H_1. The lack of any overlap between the two estimated distributions indicates that the signal can be detected almost all the time even when the false alarm probability is very low. (Setting the detection threshold at the maximum observed value of the GLRT under H_0 gives a false alarm probability of $\approx 1/500$ given the number of H_0 data realizations used here.)

Both the parameter estimation and detection results tell us that PSO is able to get us a performance that is quite satisfactory given that its computational cost is lower than any reasonable grid-based search. (Note that with proper tuning, one can bring the cost of PSO down further.)

It should be noted here that each fitness evaluation in PSO incurs the extra computational cost of generating a quadratic chirp on the fly, which can be avoided for a grid-based search with a fixed grid by generating and storing the quadratic chirps in advance. However, storing and efficiently retrieving such a large number of vectors from memory or disc, not to mention the time taken to initialize them, can lead to inefficiencies. A true comparison of computational costs, therefore,

---

[1]Of course, smarter strategies for placing the grid are conceivable that can reduce the number of points. However, these would rapidly fail as the number of parameters increases.

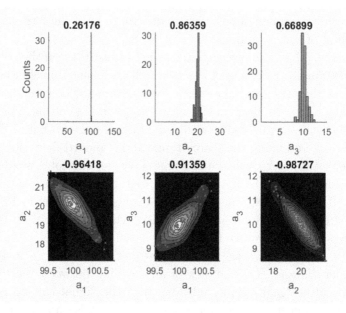

Figure 5.3 (Top row) Histograms of estimated values of a_1, a_2, and a_3 obtained from 100 data realizations under H_1. The red line in each plot indicates the true parameter value. The range of the horizontal axis in each histogram is the search range used in PSO for the corresponding parameter: $[10, 150]$, $[1, 30]$, and $[1, 15]$ for a_1, a_2, and a_3 respectively. The error in a_1 is so small that the width of the histogram for a_1 is nearly equal to that of the line showing the true parameter value, making it difficult to resolve the details. The number at the top of each panel is the standard deviation of the estimated values. (Bottom row) Scatterplots of a_i and a_j, for all combinations of i and $j \neq i$. The number at the top of each panel is the Pearson Correlation Coefficient [51] for the scatterplot. The high values of correlation coefficient (which is always limited to $[-1, 1]$) show that the estimation errors in the different parameters are not independent but highly correlated for the quadratic chirp. The background of each scatterplot is a contour map of the bivariate pdf estimated from the data points. The true signal in the simulated data under H_1 has SNR $= 10$, $a_1 = 100$, $a_2 = 20$, and $a_3 = 10$.

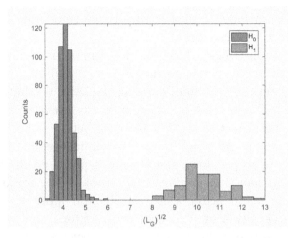

Figure 5.4 Histograms of the square root of the GLRT (L_G) for the quadratic chirp . The H_0 histogram was obtained with 500 and the H_1 histogram with 100 data realizations.

requires a measurement of the *computation time* of a given method. The curious reader may wish to undertake this as an exercise!

5.3 NON-PARAMETRIC REGRESSION

The minimal performance condition (Sec. 5.2.1) used for tuning PSO in parametric regression – where the true signal parameters are known – is not a practical one to use for tuning in non-parametric regression. This is because the latter is designed to capture a larger class of signals and it may not be possible to express all these signals in terms of a parametrized form with a fixed number of parameters. Moreover, one does not expect a non-parametric method to reproduce every feature of any given signal. Therefore, it is not possible to compare the fitness found by PSO with the fitness at the "true location" because the former will almost always be worse. On the other hand, a consistently better fitness from PSO may simply be an indication of overfitting and not necessarily a better fit to the true signal.

One straightforward option for tuning PSO for non-parametric regression is to increase N_{iter} and N_{runs} to the largest value one can afford based on available computational resources. This brute-force strategy works because we know that the performance of PSO becomes better as both these numbers go up. Although the relative influence of N_{runs} and N_{iter} is hard to pin down exactly and depends on the fitness function at hand, a smarter strategy that often works is to have N_{runs} be the same as the available number of parallel workers (usually 4 or 8 in high end desktops) and increase N_{iter} until a reasonable performance is achieved across a sufficiently broad range of signal shapes.

If one finds that increasing N_{iter} for a moderately large value of N_{runs} (≈ 12 or less) does not yield good performance, it is usually worth taking a second look at the variant of PSO being used or the formulation of the problem itself. If sources of degeneracies in the fitness function can be identified, it is best to reformulate the problem, using reparametrization for example, to remove them before pushing PSO to the extreme. Reparametrization in the context of the regression spline method is discussed next.

5.3.1 Reparametrization in regression spline

The parameters in the regression spline method that constitute the search space for PSO are the M breakpoints $\bar{b} = (b_0, b_1, \ldots, b_{M-1})$. The spline that is subtracted from the data when evaluating the least squares function is a linear combination of B-splines determined by $\bar{b}$ (see Eq. 1.11).

There is a clear source of parametric degeneracy if one were to use the components of $\bar{b}$ itself as the parameters for PSO to search over: Since particles can move in an unconstrained way in this space, it is possible for two particles to be at locations that simply correspond to a permutation of the elements of $\bar{b}$. (For example, consider the case where the two locations are

$(b_0 = 1, b_1 = 2, b_2 = 3, \ldots)$ and $(b_0 = 2, b_1 = 3, b_2 = 1, \ldots)$ with all b_i, $i \geq 3$ being equal.) However, any sequence of breakpoints must be sorted before it is used in the construction of B-splines, making the splines corresponding to the two locations above identical. Consequently, these two particles will have the same fitness values. Extending this simple example to all the particle locations in this space, it is easy to see that there is a huge scope for degeneracies in the fitness function. Such a fitness function would be extremely difficult for any stochastic optimization method to handle as it would be very rugged due to the numerous local minima with identical values.

To cure the source of degeneracy identified above, an obvious solution is to enforce monotonicity in the breakpoint sequence. That is, ensure that $b_{i+1} > b_i$. But this makes the shape of the search space non-hypercubical. As mentioned earlier in Sec. 4.5, PSO is known to work best when the shape of the search space is a hypercube. Hence, curing the degeneracy problem in this way will open a different, perhaps equally nasty, problem.

There is a different way to maintain monotonicity of the breakpoints while maintaining the hypercubical shape of the search space. The solution is to change from $\bar{b}$ to a new set of parameters, $\bar{\gamma}$, defined as follows.

$$\gamma_0 = \frac{b_0 - x_0}{T}, \tag{5.6}$$

$$\gamma_i = \frac{b_i - b_{i-1}}{x_{N-1} - b_{i-1}} \quad \text{for } i = 1, 2, \ldots, M - 1 \ , \tag{5.7}$$

where $T = x_{N-1} - x_0$. It follows that for $0 \leq \gamma_i \leq 1$, $b_{i+1} > b_i$ and $\bar{b}$ is monotonic. In addition, each γ_i can be varied independently of the others over the range $[0, 1]$, making the search space a hypercube. Hence, this reparametrization solves both the monotonicity and the search space shape requirements.

While it solves the two main problems identified above, it turns out that this particular reparametrization is not conducive to extracting a good performance from PSO. The reason is that one expects the uniformly spaced breakpoint sequence, where $b_{i+1} - b_i$ is a constant, to be of special importance in a spline-based smoothing method. In particular, if the true signal is not concentrated in a small section of the interval $[x_0, x_{N-1}]$, one would expect that the best fit spline would have nearly uniformly spaced points.

In the above reparametrization, a uniformly spaced breakpoint sequence corresponds to $\gamma_i \propto 1/(x_{N-1} - b_{i-1})$ and, hence, γ_i increases as i (and b_{i-1}) increase. This means that the uniformly spaced breakpoint sequence corresponds to a point in the new parameters that is displaced strongly from the center of the hypercubical search space. One would like to avoid this situation because it would result in a poor performance of PSO – particles near the boundary tend to exit the search space more often and convergence to a breakpoint sequence that is approximately uniform would be harder.

It turns out that the latter problem can also be solved by slightly altering the definition of $\overline{\gamma}$ as follows.

$$\gamma_0 = \frac{b_0 - x_0}{T}, \tag{5.8}$$

$$\gamma_i = \frac{b_i - b_{i-1}}{b_{i+1} - b_{i-1}}, \quad \text{for } 1 \le i \le M - 2, \tag{5.9}$$

$$\gamma_{M-1} = \frac{b_{M-1} - b_0}{x_{N-1} - b_0}. \tag{5.10}$$

In the above reparametrization, setting $\gamma_i = 0.5$ for $1 \le i \le M - 2$ generates a breakpoint sequence where b_i, $1 \le i \le M - 2$, are uniformly spaced. Hence, the uniformly spaced sequence (at least up to the interior breakpoints) is now closer to the center of the search space (where $\gamma_i \in [0, 1]$, $\forall i$).

In order to evaluate the fitness function, $\overline{\gamma}$ must be inverted to give the actual breakpoint sequence $\overline{b}$. For Eqs. 5.6 and 5.7, this inversion can be performed iteratively starting with the inversion of b_0 from γ_0. For the parameters defined in Eqs. 5.8 to 5.10, the system of equations relating $\overline{\gamma}$ and $\overline{b}$ is of the form[2] $\mathbf{A}(\overline{\gamma})\overline{b}^T = \overline{c}^T(\overline{\gamma})$, allowing $\overline{b}$ to be solved by inverting $\mathbf{A}(\overline{\gamma})$.

---

[2]The reader can easily work out the matrices $\mathbf{A}(\overline{\gamma})$ and $\overline{c}(\overline{\gamma})$ from the defining equations for $\overline{\gamma}$.

5.3.2   Results: Fixed number of breakpoints

Having reparametrized the breakpoints as defined by Eqs. 5.8 to 5.10, we can proceed to characterize the performance of the regression spline method. First, we will do this for a fixed, and the smallest possible, number of breakpoints for a cubic B-spline: $\overline{\gamma} = (\gamma_0, \gamma_1, \ldots, \gamma_{M-1})$ with $M = 5$. This matches the case of the true signal described in Eq. 1.12, which is simply a single B-spline.

In order to see if the optimization over breakpoints is essential, let us also consider the case where they are not optimized but spaced uniformly. B-splines constructed out of uniformly spaced breakpoints are called *cardinal* B-splines and we call a linear combination of such B-splines a *cardinal spline*. The fitness function for a cardinal spline remains the same as the one used in regression spline except that there is no minimization over breakpoints after that over the spline coefficients $\overline{\alpha}$.

Fig. 5.5 shows the estimated signals, for one data realization, obtained from the regression spline method and for a cardinal spline. The same number, $M = 5$, of breakpoints is used in both cases. It is clear from just a visual inspection that the solution obtained by optimizing the breakpoints is far better, in terms of its agreement with the true signal, than the one obtained using fixed breakpoints. Here, we have used $N_{\text{runs}} = 4$ and $N_{\text{iter}} = 200$ for PSO with all other settings kept as shown in Table 4.2 for lbest PSO.

A numerical issue arises in evaluating the fitness function when two or more breakpoints come closer than the spacing between the values of the independent variable. This can lead to the analytical minimization over the B-spline coefficients, $\overline{\alpha}$, becoming ill-posed. A simple way to mitigate this problem is to trap such anomalous breakpoint sequences before they are passed on to the fitness function and move apart the breakpoints that are too close to a preset minimum distance. If the minimum distance is set to be the minimum separation between the independent variable values, the ill-posedness is

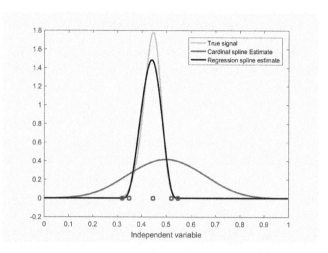

Figure 5.5 The true signal (gray) and the ones estimated by regression spline (black) and cardinal spline (blue) methods. The square markers show the breakpoints optimized by PSO.

resolved. This extra operation alters the fitness value slightly in those parts of the search space that contain the pathological breakpoint sequences, but it does not affect the overall performance of the method in the bulk of the search space.

5.3.3 Results: Variable number of breakpoints

In order to be of any use in the general situation where the true signal is not as simple as the one used in this book, the regression spline method must use a variable number of breakpoints. One way to incorporate a variable number of breakpoints is to perform model selection for which we use the *Akaike Information Criterion* (AIC) defined below.

Let $\widehat{L}_P(\mathbb{T})$ be the maximum value of the log-likelihood function, for given data $\mathbb{T}$, over the parameters $\bar{\theta} = (\theta_0, \theta_1, \ldots, \theta_{P-1})$ of a regression model with P parameters. Then

$$\text{AIC} \; = \; 2P - 2\widehat{L}_P(\mathbb{T}) \,. \tag{5.11}$$

With an increase in P, a model will be better able to fit the data and $\widehat{L}_P(\mathbb{T})$ will increase and AIC will decrease. However, at some point the improvement in the fit will slacken off, allowing the first term to take over and AIC will start to increase. The model selected is the value of P at which AIC attains a minimum.

In the context of regression spline, P is the number of breakpoints used. Thus, model selection in this case means applying regression spline to the *same* data realization with different numbers of breakpoints, $M \in \{M_1, M_2, \ldots, M_K\}$, and picking the optimal value of M using AIC. The set of K values of the number of breakpoints to use has to be specified by the analyst and, hence, is somewhat subjective. Nonetheless, it is much easier to specify a reasonable list of values for M rather than guess one particular optimal value. Moreover, it allows the regression spline method to adapt better to the true signal present in the data.

However, the direct use of AIC results in a new problem. As the number of breakpoints increases in the regression spline method, so does its tendency to cluster them together in order to fit outliers in the data rather than fit a smooth signal. Since the presence of noise can result in many such outliers, model selection alone tends to favor models with higher breakpoint numbers so that such outliers can be removed. In order to counter this and force the method to seek smooth solutions, which is the behavior we expect from the signals of interest, we need to regularize the method. This can be done by adding a term to the fitness function that penalizes undesirable solutions.

Since the clustering of breakpoints conspires with high values for the B-spline coefficients $\overline{\alpha}$ in order to fit outliers, one possibility is to impose a penalty,

$$R(\overline{\alpha}) = \overline{\alpha}\overline{\alpha}^T = \sum_{i=0}^{M-1} \alpha_i^2 . \tag{5.12}$$

on the B-spline coefficients themselves. The fitness function to be minimized becomes

$$L_S^R = L_S + \lambda R(\overline{\alpha}) , \qquad (5.13)$$

where L_S is the original fitness function of the regression spline method. Here, $\lambda \geq 0$ is a constant called the *regulator gain* which governs the effect of the penalty term on the solution. For $\lambda = 0$, the original fitness function is recovered. As $\lambda \to \infty$, the solution tries to minimize only $R(\overline{\alpha})$, in which case $\alpha_i \to 0$, $\forall i$, leading to an estimated signal that is zero everywhere. (The derivation of l_S provided in Sec. C.2 can easily be extended to include the penalty term and is left as an exercise.)

Fig. 5.6 shows a comparison of the regularized regression spline method with the cardinal spline fit. It is clear that the optimization of breakpoints leads to better results again. The settings used for PSO here remain the same as in Sec. 5.3.2: $N_{\text{runs}} = 4$ and $N_{\text{iter}} = 200$ with all other settings kept as in Table 4.2 for lbest PSO.

The results in Fig. 5.6 for the cardinal spline fit method have been derived without regularization ($\lambda = 0$). One observes that the estimated signals have a systematic shift towards a lower peak amplitude. Using regularization will only make matters worse for this method as the estimated signals will be pushed down further in amplitude.

While we have chosen the regulator gain for regression spline somewhat arbitrarily here, there exist methods, such as *cross-validation*, that may be used to find an optimum value for it. We do not extend the discussion further on this topic as it will take us well outside the scope of this book.

Finally, Fig. 5.7 shows the distributions of the GLRT under H_0 and H_1. We see that the two distributions are well separated at the SNR used for the true signal.

5.4 NOTES AND SUMMARY

The terminology used in Sec. 5.1.2 for describing the simulated data is derived from the field of time-domain signal

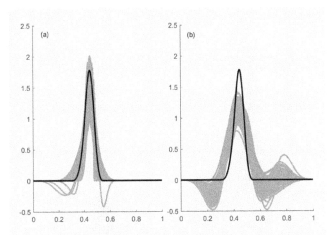

Figure 5.6 The estimated signals from (a) the regularized regression spline method, and (b) cardinal spline fit for 100 data realizations. The true signal in all the realizations is the one shown in black. It follows Eq. 1.12 and has SNR = 10. All the estimated signals are plotted together in gray. Model selection was used in both cases with the number of breakpoints $K \in \{5, 6, 7, 8, 9\}$. The regulator gain in the case of the regression spline method was set at $\lambda = 5.0$. For the cardinal spline fit, $\lambda = 0$.

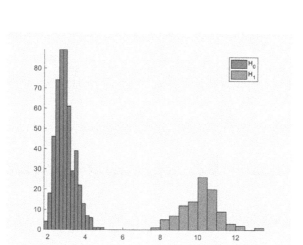

Figure 5.7 Histograms of the square root of the GLRT (L_G) for the regularized regression spline method with model selection. The number of breakpoints used were $M \in \{5, 6, 7, 8, 9\}$ and the regulator gain was set at $\lambda = 5.0$. The H_0 histogram was obtained with 500 and the H_1 histogram with 100 data realizations.

processing [21]. The minimal performance condition was proposed as a figure of merit for quantifying the performance of PSO in [48]. Its use in the metric for tuning defined in Eq. 5.5 is formalized in [35]. The reparametrization of breakpoints in Eq. 5.8 to 5.10 was introduced in [32]. A reference text for model selection is [6]. The penalty term in Eq. 5.12 is the basis of the penalized spline approach discussed in [42]. (This text also contains references to the literature on cross-validation.) An example of a regression method where both AIC-based model selection and cross-validation are used can be found in [33].

5.4.1 Summary

In this concluding chapter we have shown how a SI method such as PSO can help open up new possibilities in statistical analysis. The computational cost of minimizing the fitness function can become infeasible even for a small search space dimensionality when a grid-based strategy is used. Traditionally, the only option for statistical analysts in such situations has been to use methods under the random sampling metaheuristic, which are not only computationally expensive and wasteful in terms of fitness evaluations, but also fairly cumbersome to tune. This has prevented many a novice user of statistical methods from venturing too far from linear models in their analysis since these lead to convex optimization problems that are easily solved. However, non-linear models are becoming increasingly prevalent and unavoidable across many application areas as the problems being tackled become progressively more complex.

Using a three dimensional non-linear parametric regression example, we showed that PSO could easily solve for the best fit model with very small computational cost (in terms of the number of fitness evaluations) while admitting a fairly robust and straightforward tuning process. The example we chose was deliberately kept simple in many ways in order to let the reader reproduce it easily. However, PSO has already been applied to many real world non-linear parametric regression problems with higher dimensionalities and found to work quite well. Some of these applications do require special tweaking of PSO, such as changing the PSO variant that is used or imposing special boundary conditions, but the effort needed to get it to work well is generally far less than that for more traditional methods.

The problem of non-linear optimization has been a major roadblock in non-parametric regression. Here, more than in the case of parametric regression, the large number of parameters has generally forced the use of linear models. At some level, of course, the number of parameters can become so large that it is best to stick to linear models. However, as shown in this book, it is possible to extract much better performance in some cases by shifting to a moderate dimensional non-linear approach than a large dimensional linear one. PSO played a critical role in allowing this shift for the regression spline method considered in this book. In this method, the search space dimensionality (number of breakpoints) went up to a large value of 9 but PSO could still handle the optimization well.

We hope that the fairly simple illustrative problems considered in this book will not only allow readers to get familiar with PSO but also act as gateways to experimenting with and learning about other SI methods. We have not had the luxury of space and time to delve into a more detailed exposition of some important issues. One of them, for example, is that of non-hypercubical search spaces: a problem known in the optimization literature as constrained searches. However, with the working vocabulary in optimization theory and SI terminology acquired from this book, the reader is well placed to start exploring the technical literature on SI and EC methods and discovering new ways of solving statistical analysis problems.

Primer on Probability Theory

CONTENTS

This is a quick – and not a mathematically rigorous – tour of a limited set of concepts from probability theory that appear in this book. The reader interested in acquiring a deep foundation in probability theory is urged to use the many excellent texts that are available (e.g., [37] and [40]).

A.1 RANDOM VARIABLE

The first concept in probability theory is that of a *random variable* X. It is a quantity whose value cannot be predicted but all of whose possible values are known. A *trial* is the process of obtaining a value of X. Thus, the *outcome* of a trial is one of the possible values of X but we cannot predict in advance of the trial what this value is going to be. The value of a random variable obtained in a trial is commonly denoted by the corresponding lower case letter (e.g., x is a trial outcome of X).

A simple example is the number that shows up in throwing a six-sided die: we cannot predict the particular value that will appear in advance of a throw but we do know that it will be an element of the set $\{1, 2, 3, 4, 5, 6\}$. Here, the action of throwing the dice is a trial and the number that shows up is an outcome. (Deliberately placing the dice to show a particular number is not a trial in the probabilistic sense!) Another example is the temperature tomorrow at noon: We cannot predict it for sure but we believe that it will be a real number between the lowest and highest sea level temperatures ever measured on Earth. The temperature measurement process is a trial and the value we obtain is an outcome of the trial.

The set $\mathbb{S}$ of possible values that X can take is called its *sample space*. A subset $\mathbb{A}$ of the sample space is called an *event*. In the case of the dice, $\mathbb{S} = \{1, 2, 3, 4, 5, 6\}$ and $\mathbb{A} = \{2, 4, 6\}$ is the event that X takes an even value. In the case of temperature, the sample space is some interval on the real line. The former type of random variable, where the sample space is finite or may be infinite but countable, is called *discrete*. The latter type is an example of a *continuous* random variable.

A.2 PROBABILITY MEASURE

Probability theory starts with assigning a number $P(\mathbb{A})$, called a *probability measure*, to every event[1] $\mathbb{A} \in \mathbb{S}$. It helps to interpret $P(\mathbb{A})$ as the "probability of any element of event $\mathbb{A}$ occurring in a trial", or "probability that X takes a value in $\mathbb{A}$". Therefore, an equivalent notation would be $P(x \in \mathbb{A})$.

The assignment of the probability measure must follow the rules below.

- $P(\Phi) = 0$, where Φ is the empty set.

- $P(\mathbb{S}) = 1$.

---

[1]The mathematically rigorous approach requires that, before a probability measure is assigned to subsets, the subsets be chosen to form a *Borel Algebra* in order to guarantee that a countable union or intersection of events is an event and the empty set is also an event.

- $P(\mathbb{A} \cup \mathbb{B}) = P(\mathbb{A}) + P(\mathbb{B}) - P(\mathbb{A} \cap \mathbb{B})$.

The LHS of the last equation can be interpreted as "the probability of any element from $\mathbb{A}$ *or* $\mathbb{B}$ occurring in a trial is ...", while the term $P(\mathbb{A} \cap \mathbb{B})$ is subtracted in order to not double-count elements that belong to both $\mathbb{A}$ and $\mathbb{B}$.

In the *Frequentist* approach to probability theory, $P(\mathbb{A})$ is supposed to be objectively assigned by performing (or imagining) N_{trials} trials and counting the number $N(\mathbb{A})$ of those trials in which the event $\mathbb{A}$ occurred. Then $P(\mathbb{A})$ is given by the frequency of occurence of $\mathbb{A}$,

$$P(\mathbb{A}) = \lim_{N_{\text{trials}} \to \infty} \frac{N(\mathbb{A})}{N_{\text{trials}}} . \tag{A.1}$$

In the *Bayesian* approach to probability theory, $P(\mathbb{A})$ is assigned subjectively according to one's *degree of belief* in $\mathbb{A}$.

Consider the sample space of a single dice as an example. The so-called *fair dice* probability measure on the sample space is given by: $P(x) = 1/6$ for $x \in \{1, 2, \ldots, 6\}$. Once the probability measure is defined on these elementary subsets, the probability for any other event then simply follows from the rules stated above. For instance, for $\mathbb{A} = \{2, 4, 6\}$,

$$\begin{aligned}
P(\mathbb{A}) &= P(\{2\} \cup \{4\} \cup \{6\}) , \\
&= P(\{2\}) + P(\{4\}) + P(\{6\}) , \\
&= \frac{1}{6} + \frac{1}{6} + \frac{1}{6} = \frac{1}{3} .
\end{aligned} \tag{A.2}$$

In the Frequentist interpretation of probability, the fair-dice measure implies that each number out of $\{1, 2, \ldots, 6\}$ appears the same number of times if the dice were, hypothetically, thrown an infinite number of times. For the same dice, everyone is supposed to agree with this measure since it is, at least in principle, verifiable.

In the Bayesian interpretation, the fair-dice measure represents our belief, independently of performing trials, that the die is constructed to be free of structural defects that favor one outcome more than the others. However, this degree of belief may not be shared by all people looking at the same dice. Some may assign an unfair dice measure for the same dice.

Once the probability measure is defined, whether in the Frequentist or Bayesian sense, the mathematical rule for obtaining the probability of any event, as illustrated in Eq. A.2, is the same in both the Frequentist and Bayesian interpretation.

A.3   JOINT PROBABILITY

The next elaboration of probability theory is the introduction of additional random variables. Let X_1 and X_2 be two random variables. If the sample space of X_i, $i = 1, 2$, is denoted by S_i, then the sample space of X_1 and X_2 is the *Cartesian product* $S_{12} = S_1 \times S_2 = \{(a_1, a_2); a_i \in S_i, i = 1, 2\}$. Take the throw of two dice as an example. The outcome of the trial is two numbers a_1 and a_2 that belong to the respective sample spaces (in this case each sample space is $\{1, 2, \ldots, 6\}$). Thus, there are two random variables here and the outcome of each trial is taken from the set $S_{12} = \{(a_1, a_2); a_i \in \{1, 2, \ldots, 6\}, i = 1, 2\}$.

As in the case of a single random variable, one can also impose a probability measure on subsets of S_{12}. This probability measure is called the *joint probability* of X_1 and X_2. To distinguish between this measure and those for X_1 and X_2 taken separately, let us use P_{12}, P_1 and P_2 for the probability measure on the subsets of S_{12}, S_1, and S_2 respectively. Since every event $A \subseteq S_{12}$ can be expressed as $A = (A_1 \subseteq S_1) \times (A_2 \subseteq S_2)$, for some A_1 and A_2, $P_{12}(A) = P_{12}(A_1 \times A_2)$ is the same as saying "probability that X_1 takes a value in A_1 *and* X_2 takes a value in A_2 **in the same trial**".

From the above statement, it follows that the probability $P_1(A_1 \subseteq S_1)$ is the "probability that X_1 takes a value in A_1 and X_2 takes **any** value in S_2 in the same trial" (i.e., we do not care what value X_2 takes in a trial). This means that $P_1(A_1) = P_{12}(A_1 \times S_2)$. Similarly, one can derive $P_2(A_2) = P_{12}(S_1 \times A_2)$. Obtaining the individual probability measure P_i of X_i from

P_{12} is called *marginalization* of the joint probability over the other random variable $X_{j \neq i}$.

Let us consider N_{trials} trials in the limit $N_{\text{trials}} \to \infty$. Then, the number of trials in which $X_1 \in \mathbb{A}$ is $N_{\text{trials}} P_1(\mathbb{A})$ and the number of trials in which $X_2 \in \mathbb{B}$ and $X_1 \in \mathbb{A}$ is $N_{\text{trials}} P_{12}(\mathbb{A} \times \mathbb{B})$. If we now confine ourselves to the subset of trials where $X_1 \in \mathbb{A}$, the measured probability of $X_2 \in \mathbb{B}$ in those trials is called the *conditional probability* $P_{2|1}(\mathbb{B}|\mathbb{A})$ of $X_2 \in \mathbb{B}$ given $X_1 \in \mathbb{A}$. Taking the ratio of the number of trials, we get

$$P_{2|1}(\mathbb{B}|\mathbb{A}) = P_{12}(\mathbb{A} \times \mathbb{B})/P_1(\mathbb{A}) . \tag{A.3}$$

Similarly, one obtains the conditional probability,

$$P_{1|2}(\mathbb{A}|\mathbb{B}) = P_{12}(\mathbb{A} \times \mathbb{B})/P_2(\mathbb{B}) , \tag{A.4}$$

of $X_1 \in \mathbb{A}$ given $X_2 \in \mathbb{B}$.

From Eq. A.3 and Eq. A.4, we get

$$
\begin{aligned}
P_{1|2}(\mathbb{A}|\mathbb{B})P_2(\mathbb{B}) &= P_{2|1}(\mathbb{B}|\mathbb{A})P_1(\mathbb{A}) , \\
\Rightarrow P_{1|2}(\mathbb{A}|\mathbb{B}) &= \frac{P_{2|1}(\mathbb{B}|\mathbb{A})P_1(\mathbb{A})}{P_2(\mathbb{B})} .
\end{aligned}
\tag{A.5}
$$

Eq. A.5 is the famous *Bayes law* in statistical inference. Loosely speaking, when X_2 and X_1 represent "data" and the "quantity to be estimated from the data" respectively, Bayes law allows us to update our *prior degree of belief*, P_1, about X_1 to a *posterior degree of belief*, $P_{1|2}$, based on some model, $P_{2|1}$, called the *likelihood*, of how the probability of X_2 is affected by different values of X_1.

It is important to understand that the conditional probability of a random variable is **not** the same as its marginal probability in general: $P_{1|2}(\mathbb{A}|\mathbb{B}) = P_1(\mathbb{A})$ only when $\mathbb{B} = \mathbb{S}_2$. However, when two random variables are *statistically independent*, $P_{1|2}(\mathbb{A}|\mathbb{B}) = P_1(\mathbb{A})$ for any $\mathbb{B}$. (Similarly, $P_{2|1}(\mathbb{B}|\mathbb{A}) = P_2(\mathbb{B})$ for any $\mathbb{A}$.) This is the mathematically proper way of stating that the probability of $X_1 \in \mathbb{A}$ is not affected by the value that X_2 takes. From the definition of conditional probability in Eq. A.3 or Eq. A.4, it follows that when X1 and X2 are statistically independent,

$$P_{12}(\mathbb{A} \times \mathbb{B}) = P_1(\mathbb{A})P_2(\mathbb{B}) , \tag{A.6}$$

in order for their respective conditional and marginal probabilities to be equal.

An example of statistical independence is given by two people in two separate rooms throwing a die each. Knowing the outcome of the throw in one room gives us no clue about the probability of getting a particular outcome in the other room. On the other hand, if one takes the temperature in a room and some measure of fatigue, such as efficiency in performing a given task, of a worker in that room, one would expect that the probability of obtaining a particular level of efficiency depends on the temperature in the room. This is an example where the value of one random variable (temperature) affects the probability of another (efficiency). Note that measuring a certain level of efficiency also tells us how probable it is for the room to be at a certain temperature. Of course, one does not expect measuring efficiency to be a good way of predicting temperature. On the other hand, measuring temperature may be a good way of predicting efficiency. This asymmetry is not an inconsistency because the two conditional probabilities are measures of different events.

A.4   CONTINUOUS RANDOM VARIABLES

From now on, we will focus on only continuous random variables. It will turn out that much of the mathematics of probability theory for discrete random variables is a special case of that for continuous ones.

When X is a continuous random variable that takes values in $\mathbb{R}$, it only makes sense to talk about the probability of an interval[2] in $\mathbb{R}$, no matter how small, rather than a single point in

---

[2]Formally, an interval in $\mathbb{R}$ is a set with the property that any number between two unequal numbers in the set is also in the set.

$\mathbb{R}$. Heuristically, this is easy to understand from the Frequentist perspective: one would have to wait an infinite number of trials before the exact real number x obtained in a given trial is obtained again. (Think of $x = \pi$ for example. One would have to do an infinite number of trials before one obtains π exact to each of its non-repeating decimal places.) Hence, in the notation of Eq. A.1, $P(\{x\}) = \lim_{N_{\text{trials}} \to \infty} N(\{x\})/N_{\text{trials}} = 0$.

Just as in the case of a die, where assigning the probability measure to elementary events $\{1\}$, $\{2\}$, etc., was sufficient to obtain the probability of any event (e.g., the subset of even numbers), it is sufficient to assign probability measures to infinitesimal intervals $[x, x + dx) \subset \mathbb{R}$ for a continuous random variable[3]. This is represented as,

$$P([x, x + dx)) \;=\; p_X(x)dx \ . \tag{A.7}$$

The function $p_X(x)$ is called the *probability density function* (pdf) of X.

Using the rules of probability theory, $P([a, b])$ for a finite interval $[a, b]$ can be obtained by breaking it up into contiguous disjoint discrete intervals and summing up the probabilities for each. This naturally leads to an integral,

$$P([a, b]) \;=\; \int_a^b p_X(x)dx \ . \tag{A.8}$$

Note that while $P([a, b]) \leq 1$, $p_X(x)$ can be greater than 1. Since the sample space of X is a subset of $\mathbb{R}$, $P(\mathbb{R}) = 1$ and

$$\int_{-\infty}^{\infty} p_X(x)dx = 1 \ . \tag{A.9}$$

Finally, since $P([a, b]) \geq 0$ for any interval, $p_X(x) \geq 0$ everywhere on $\mathbb{R}$.

From the properties of $p_X(x)$, it follows that if $P([a, b]) = 0$ then $p_X(x) = 0$ for $x \in [a, b]$. This allows us to treat the sample space of any continuous random variable to be the whole of $\mathbb{R}$

---

[3] $[x, x + dx)$ denotes an interval that includes x but not $x + dx$.

even if the actual sample space is a proper subset $\mathbb{S} \subset \mathbb{R}$. We simply set $p_X(x) = 0$ for $x \notin \mathbb{S}$, ensuring that X never gets a value outside $\mathbb{S}$ in any trial.

By introducing the *Dirac delta function*, $\delta(x)$, defined by

$$\int_a^b dx \delta(x-c)f(x) = \begin{cases} f(c), & a < c < b, \\ 0, & \text{otherwise} \end{cases} ,\text{(A.10)}$$

one can subsume the case of a discrete random variable into the probability theory of a continuous one. If the probability measure for each element x_i, $i = 1, 2, \ldots$, of the sample space of a discrete random variable is $P(x_i)$, then $p_X(x) = \sum_{i=1}^N P(x_i)\delta(x - x_i)$ as can be verified directly by integrating $p_X(x)$ in any finite interval.

The next step is the introduction of the *joint probability density function* (joint pdf) $p_{X_1 X_2}(x, y)$ of two continuous random variables X and Y. The sample space of X and Y is $\mathbb{R}^2 = \mathbb{R} \times \mathbb{R}$, namely the 2-dimensional plane. If one takes an area $\mathbb{A} \subset \mathbb{R}^2$, then

$$P_{12}(\mathbb{A}) = \int_{\mathbb{A}} dx dy p_{XY}(x, y) . \tag{A.11}$$

From the joint pdf, one can derive the pdf of any one of the variables by marginalization.

$$\begin{aligned} P_1([a, b]) &= \int_a^b p_X(x) dx = P_{12}([a, b] \times \mathbb{R}) , \\ &= \int_a^b dx \int_{-\infty}^{\infty} dy p_{XY}(x, y) , \\ \Rightarrow p_X(x) &= \int_{-\infty}^{\infty} dy p_{XY}(x, y) . \end{aligned} \tag{A.12}$$

The conditional probability of $x \in \mathbb{A}$ given $y \in \mathbb{B}$ is given by

$$P_{1|2}(\mathbb{A}|\mathbb{B}) = \frac{\int_{\mathbb{A} \times \mathbb{B}} p_{XY}(x, y) dx dy}{\int_{\mathbb{B}} p_Y(y) dy} . \tag{A.13}$$

If $\mathbb{B} = [y, y + \epsilon)$, where ϵ is infinitesimally small, then the denominator is $p_Y(y)\epsilon$ and the numerator is $\epsilon \int_\mathbb{A} p_{XY}(x,y)dx$, which gives

$$P_{1|2}(\mathbb{A}|[y, y + \epsilon)) = \int_\mathbb{A} dx \frac{p_{XY}(x,y)}{p_Y(y)} \qquad (\text{A.14})$$

This motivates the definition of the conditional pdf,

$$p_{X|Y}(x|y) = \frac{p_{XY}(x,y)}{p_Y(y)}, \qquad (\text{A.15})$$

giving $P_{1|2}(\mathbb{A}|[y, y + \epsilon)) = \int_\mathbb{A} dx p_{X|Y}(x|y)$.

All the above definitions for two continuous random variables extend easily to N random variables $\overline{X} = (X_0, X_1, \ldots, X_{N-1})$.

Joint pdf: $p_{\overline{X}}(\overline{x})$ defined by

$$P_{12\ldots N}(\mathbb{A}) = \int_\mathbb{A} d^N x p_{\overline{X}}(\overline{x}) . \qquad (\text{A.16})$$

Conditional pdf: $p_{\overline{X}|\overline{Y}}(\overline{x}|\overline{y})$ where $\overline{x} \in \mathbb{R}^N$ and $\overline{y} \in \mathbb{R}^M$ and $N \neq M$ in general.

$$p_{\overline{X}|\overline{Y}}(\overline{x}|\overline{y}) = \frac{p_{\overline{X}\overline{Y}}(\overline{x}, \overline{y})}{p_{\overline{Y}}(\overline{y})} . \qquad (\text{A.17})$$

In the special case where X_i is statistically independent of X_j, for $i \neq j$, the joint pdf becomes,

$$\begin{aligned} p_{\overline{X}}(\overline{x}) &= p_{X_0}(x_0)p_{X_1}(x_1)\ldots p_{X_{N-1}}(x_{N-1}) , \\ &= \Pi_{i=0}^{N-1} p_{X_i}(x_i) . \end{aligned} \qquad (\text{A.18})$$

A.5 EXPECTATION

With the probabilistic description of a continuous random variable in hand, we can introduce some additional useful concepts.

Expectation: $E[f(X)]$, where $f(x)$ is a function, defined by

$$E[f(X)] = \int_{-\infty}^{\infty} dx f(x) p_X(x) . \qquad (\text{A.19})$$

Some expectations have a special significance in probability theory. Among these is the nth *central moment* defined by $E[(X - E[X])^n]$ for $n > 1$. $E[X]$ itself is called the *mean* of the pdf, while the 2nd central moment is called the *variance*. The square root of the variance is called the *standard deviation* of the pdf.

The definition of expectation can be generalized to more than one random variables,

$$E[f(X, Y)] \;=\; \int_{-\infty}^{\infty} \int_{-\infty}^{\infty} dx\, dy\, f(x, y) p_{XY}(x, y) \;.\text{(A.20)}$$

$E[(X - E[X])(Y - E[Y])]$ for two random variables X and Y is called their *covariance*. Note that the covariance of a random variable with itself is simply its variance. It is easily shown that if X and Y are statistically independent, their covariance is zero. However, the opposite is not true: a covariance of zero does not necessarily mean statistical independence.

Another type of expectation that can be defined in the case of two random variables is the **conditional expectation**: $E_{X|Y}[f(X)|y]$ is defined by

$$E_{X|Y}[f(X)|y] \;=\; \int_{-\infty}^{\infty} dx\, f(x) p_{X|Y}(x|y) \;. \qquad \text{(A.21)}$$

The different types of expectations discussed above simply differ in the pdf – marginal, joint, or conditional – inside the integrand.

A.6   COMMON PROBABILITY DENSITY FUNCTIONS

In this book, we encounter (i) the *normal* (also called *Gaussian*) pdf,

$$p_X(x; \mu, \sigma) \;=\; \frac{1}{\sqrt{2\pi}\sigma} \exp\left(\frac{1}{2\sigma^2}(x - \mu)^2 \right) \;, \qquad \text{(A.22)}$$

where the two parameters μ and σ correspond to the mean and standard deviation of X respectively, and (ii) the *uniform* pdf,

$$p_X(x; a, b) = \begin{cases} \frac{1}{b-a}, & a \le x \le b \\ 0, & \text{otherwise} \end{cases} . \quad (A.23)$$

The normal pdf is common enough that a special symbol, $N(x; \mu, \sigma)$, is often used to denote it. The symbol used for the uniform pdf is $U(x; a, b)$. (A random variable with a normal or uniform pdf is said to be *normally* or *uniformly* distributed.)

Two random variables X_0 and X_1 are said to have a *bivariate normal* pdf if,

$$p_{XY}(x, y) = \frac{1}{2\pi |\mathbf{C}|^{1/2}} \exp\left(-\frac{1}{2}\|\bar{x} - \bar{\mu}\|^2\right), \quad (A.24)$$

where for any vector $\bar{z} \in \mathbb{R}^2$,

$$\|\bar{z}\|^2 = \begin{pmatrix} z_0 & z_1 \end{pmatrix} \mathbf{C}^{-1} \begin{pmatrix} z_0 \\ z_1 \end{pmatrix}, \quad (A.25)$$

$\bar{\mu} = (\mu_0, \mu_1)$ contains the mean values of X_0 and X_1 respectively, and C_{ij}, for $i, j \in \{0, 1\}$, is the covariance of X_i and X_j. The symbol $|\mathbf{C}|$ denotes the determinant of $\mathbf{C}$.

The generalization of the bivariate normal pdf to more than two random variables is called the *multivariate normal* pdf. It is given by the same expression as Eq. A.24 but with $\bar{x} = (x_0, x_1, \ldots, x_{N-1})$, $\bar{\mu}_i = E[X_i]$, and $\mathbf{C}$ being an $N \times N$ matrix of covariances between each pair of random variables. In particular, for $\mathbf{C} = \sigma^2 \mathbf{I}$, where $\mathbf{I}$ is the identity matrix,

$$\begin{aligned} p_{\bar{X}}(\bar{x}) &= \frac{1}{(\sqrt{2\pi})^N \sigma^N} \exp\left(-\frac{1}{2} \sum_{i=0}^{N-1} \frac{(x_i - \mu)^2}{\sigma^2}\right), \\ &= \Pi_{i=0}^{N-1} N(x_i; \mu, \sigma), \end{aligned} \quad (A.26)$$

is the joint pdf of identically and independently distributed (*iid*) normal random variables.

A thorough description of useful and common univariate and multivariate pdfs can be found in [23] and [30] respectively. The properties of the multivariate normal pdf are discussed in the context of statistical analysis in [1].

[9]

Splines

CONTENTS

Splines form an important class of functions in non-parametric regression problems where the regression model needs to be flexible while satisfying a smoothness condition. Spline based models also allow some useful constraints to be imposed in addition to smoothness. This appendix summarizes some basic concepts related to splines that are sufficient to understand the material in the book. The reader may consult sources such as [10] and [42, 47] for an exhaustive review of splines and spline-based regression respectively.

B.1   DEFINITION

Consider data that is in the form $\{(b_i, y_i)\}$, $i = 0, 1, \ldots, M-1$, where $b_{i+1} > b_i$ are called *breakpoints*. A spline, $f(x)$, is a piece-wise polynomial function defined over the interval $x \in [b_0, b_{M-1}]$ such that for $j = 1, \ldots, M - 1$,

$$f(x) = g^{(j)}(x) , x \in [b_{j-1}, b_j] , \qquad (B.1)$$

$$g^{(j)}(x) = \sum_{r=1}^{k} a_r^{(j)}(x - b_{j-1})^{r-1} , \qquad (B.2)$$

$$g^{(j)}(b_j) = y_j , \qquad (B.3)$$

$$g^{(j)}(b_{j-1}) = y_{j-1} , \qquad (B.4)$$

where k is the *order* of the polynomial pieces, and for $m = 1, \ldots, M - 2$, and $n = 1, \ldots, k - 2$,

$$\frac{d^n g^{(m)}}{dx^n}\bigg|_{x=b_m} = \frac{d^n g^{(m+1)}}{dx^n}\bigg|_{x=b_m}. \tag{B.5}$$

Splines are more commonly referred to in terms of the degree of the polynomial pieces rather than their order. Thus, for $k = 4$ the polynomial pieces are cubic and the corresponding spline $f(x)$ is called a *cubic spline*. Similarly, for $k = 2$, one has the *linear spline*.

In words, Eq. B.1 states that $f(x)$ is composed of polynomials defined over the disjoint intervals $[b_{j-1}, b_j]$, $j = 1, 2, \ldots, M - 1$. Eq. B.2 defines a polynomial piece where we see the as yet undetermined coefficients $a_r^{(j)}$ defining the polynomial. Eqs. B.3 to B.5 are the conditions, all defined at the breakpoints, that determine the polynomial coefficients. The conditions enforce that $f(x)$ matches the data at each breakpoint, $f(b_j) = y_j$, and that all its derivatives up to order $k - 2$ are continuous across each interior breakpoint b_j, $j = 1, 2, \ldots, M - 2$. (The derivatives of $f(x)$ are automatically continuous at any point between breakpoints since $g^{(j)}(x)$ are polynomials.) Thus, $f(x)$ interpolates the supplied data points with some prescribed degree of smoothness that is determined by the order of the polynomial pieces.

The basic concept of a spline can be generalized to data where there are multiple identical breakpoints. In this case, $b_{i+1} \geq b_i$, and the sequence $(b_0, b_1, \ldots, b_{M-1})$ is called the *knot sequence*. In this book, we do not consider knot sequences that are not breakpoint sequences. However, knots are very useful in general because they allow splines to approximate functions that are discontinuous in their values or in their derivatives.

Counting all the conditions from Eq. B.3 to Eq. B.5, we get $2(M - 1) + (k - 2)(M - 2) = kM - 2(k - 1)$ conditions for a total of $k(M - 1)$ unknowns, namely, the set of coefficients $\{a_r^{(j)}\}$, $j = 1, 2, \ldots, M - 1$, $r = 1, 2, \ldots, k$. Thus, there is a deficit of $k - 2$ conditions in getting a unique solution for the coefficients.

The extra conditions used to fill the deficit lead to different types of splines for the same data. For the case of cubic splines, where there are two extra conditions, some of the popular choices are as follows[1].

Natural spline: The second derivatives of $f(x)$ are zero at the two end breakpoints, $f''(b_0) = 0 = f''(b_{M-1})$.

Clamped spline: The first derivatives of $f(x)$ are set to some user-specified values, $f'(b_0) = a$ and $f'(b_{M-1}) = b$.

Periodic spline: Applicable when $y_0 = y_{M-1}$ with the conditions being $f'(b_0) = f'(b_{M-1})$ and $f''(b_0) = f''(b_{M-1})$.

Not-a-knot spline: The conditions are based on the continuity of third derivatives at the first and last interior breakpoints, $g^{(1)'''}(b_1) = g^{(2)'''}(b_1)$ and $g^{(M-2)'''}(b_{M-2}) = g^{(M-1)'''}(b_{M-2})$.

B.2 B-SPLINE BASIS

For a fixed set of M breakpoints $\bar{b} = (b_0, b_1, \ldots, b_{M-1})$, the set of all splines of order k defined by $\bar{b}$ and all possible values of $\bar{y} = (y_0, y_1, \ldots, y_{M-1})$ is a linear vector space. This simply follows from the fact that a linear combination of two splines from this set is another piecewise polynomial of the same order corresponding to the same breakpoints, hence another spline from the same set.

If no conditions are imposed on the polynomial in each interval $[b_i, b_{i+1}]$, $i = 0, 1, \ldots, M - 2$, the dimensionality of the space of piecewise polynomical functions for a given $\bar{b}$ is $k(M - 1)$. This is because the polynomial in each of the $M - 1$ intervals is a linear combination of k independent functions. Imposing continuity and differentiability conditions at the $M - 2$ interior breakpoints – with $k - 1$ conditions for a polynomial of order k – reduces the number of free parameters

---

[1]Here, a superscript prime on $f(x)$ denotes differentiation with respect to x: $f'(x) = df/dx$, $f''(x) = d^2f/dx^2$ and so on.

to $k(M-1)-(M-2)(k-1) = M+k-2$. Since these parameters uniquely label each element of the spline vector space, this is also its dimensionality if no further conditions are imposed. As discussed in the Sec. B.1, one is left with $k-2$ conditions over and above those given in Eqs. B.1 to B.5. If these conditions are imposed, usually in the form of boundary conditions such as the ones listed in Sec. B.1, the dimensionality of the space of splines drops to M.

The set of *Basis spline* (B-spline) functions, denoted by $B_{i,k}(x;\bar{b})$, $i = 0, 1, \ldots, M+k-3$, constitutes a very useful basis for the vector space of splines (without boundary conditions) described above. As such, any member, $f(x)$, of this space can be expressed as a linear combination,

$$f(x) = \sum_{i=0}^{M+k-3} \alpha_i B_{i,k}(x;\bar{b}) . \tag{B.6}$$

The B-spline basis functions can be derived from the Cox-de Boor recursion relations [9] given below. The recursions start with B-splines of order 1, which are piecewise constant functions, and build up B-splines of a higher order using the ones from the previous order. While the recursion relations can utilize any knot sequence, we will present them here for the special case where a breakpoint sequence $\bar{b} = (b_0 < b_1 < \ldots < b_{M-1})$ is given.

First, a knot sequence $\bar{\tau}$ is constructed by prepending and appending $k-1$ copies of b_0 and b_{M-1} respectively to $\bar{b}$. The recursion is initialized for $k' = 1$ by

$$B_{i,k'}(x;\bar{b}) = \begin{cases} 1, & \tau_i <= x < \tau_{i+1} \\ 0 & \text{else} \end{cases} . \tag{B.7}$$

For $2 \leq k' \leq k$,

$$B_{i,k'}(x;\bar{b}) = \frac{x - \tau_i}{\tau_{i+k'-1} - \tau_i} B_{i,k'-1}(x;\bar{b}) + \frac{\tau_{i+k'} - t}{\tau_{i+k'} - \tau_{i+1}} B_{i+1,k'-1}(x;\bar{b}) . \tag{B.8}$$

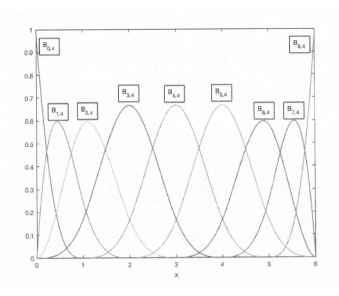

Figure B.1   The B-spline functions for an order 4 spline (cubic spline) with uniformly spaced breakpoints. The breakpoints are $\bar{b} = (b_0, b_1, \ldots, b_6)$ with $b_i = i$. If $B_{0,4}$ and $B_{8,4}$ are dropped from the basis set, the span of the remaining B-splines is a subspace of dimensionality 7 in the full 9-dimensional space of splines defined by $\bar{b}$.

For each k', $0 \leq i \leq 2(k-1) + M - (k'+1)$. From Eq. B.7, $B_{i,1}(x; \bar{b}) = 0$ when $\tau_i = t = \tau_{i+1}$, which sets any term in Eq. B.8 that has a zero in the denominator (due to knot multiplicity) to zero. Fig. B.1 illustrates B-splines for the case $k = 4$ (cubic spline) and uniformly spaced breakpoints.

For $k = 4$ (cubic splines), we can reduce the dimensionality of the vector space of splines by $k - 2 = 2$. If this is done by dropping $B_{0,4}(x; \bar{b})$ and $B_{M+1,4}(x; \bar{b})$ from the basis set constructed as above, $f(x)$ will go continuously to zero at b_0 and b_{M-1} but will have discontinuous first and second derivatives at both the locations. The splines defined in Eq. 1.10 follow from this approach.

Analytical Minimization

CONTENTS

As discussed in Sec. 5.1.1, the minimization of the fitness function in a statistical regression problem should be nested in a way that, if applicable, the inner minimization is carried out analytically. Here, we derive the form of the fitness function in the outer minimization for the parametric and non-parametric regression examples in Sec. 1.3.1 and Sec. 1.3.2 respectively. In each case, we start with the least squares function, L_S, and minimize it analytically over the parameters that appear linearly. The resulting function, l_S, is the one that is then minimized numerically.

In the following, we will use the notation

$$\langle \overline{x}, \overline{y} \rangle = \sum_{i=0}^{N-1} x_i y_i = \overline{x}\, \overline{y}^T \, , \tag{C.1}$$

$$\|\overline{x}\|^2 = \langle \overline{x}, \overline{x} \rangle \, . \tag{C.2}$$

For $\overline{x} \in \mathbb{R}^N$ and $\overline{y} \in \mathbb{R}^N$.

C.1 QUADRATIC CHIRP

The parameters of the regression model are $\bar{\theta} = (A, a_1, a_2, a_3)$ and L_S is given by Eq. 1.8. Before proceeding further, it is convenient to replace A by a redefined parameter ρ as follows. Let us express the quadratic chirp as

$$q_c(X) = Ag(X) , \tag{C.3}$$
$$g(X) = \sin(2\pi\phi(X)) . \tag{C.4}$$

Using $\bar{q}_c$ and $\bar{g}$ to denote $(q_x(x_0), q_x(x_1), \ldots, q_c(x_{N-1}))$ and $(g(x_0), g(x_1), \ldots, g(x_{N-1}))$ respectively, we get

$$\bar{q}_c = A\|\bar{g}\|\frac{\bar{g}}{\|\bar{g}\|} = \rho\bar{u} , \tag{C.5}$$

where, by definition, $\|\bar{u}\| = 1$ and $\bar{u}$ only depends on $\bar{\theta}' = (a_1, a_2, a_3)$.

Expressing L_S in terms of the redefined quantities, we get

$$\begin{aligned} L_S &= \frac{1}{2\sigma^2}\|\bar{y} - \rho\bar{u}\|^2 , \\ &= \frac{1}{2\sigma^2}\left[\|\bar{y}\|^2 - 2\rho\langle\bar{y},\bar{u}\rangle + \rho^2\right] . \end{aligned} \tag{C.6}$$

Let $\hat{\rho}$ be the minimizer of L_S over ρ keeping the other parameters fixed. Using the standard condition for the extremum of a function, we get

$$\left.\frac{\partial L_S}{\partial\rho}\right|_{\hat{\rho}} = 0 \quad \Rightarrow \quad \hat{\rho} = \langle\bar{y},\bar{u}\rangle . \tag{C.7}$$

Substituting $\hat{\rho}$ into Eq. C.6 gives us the fitness function l_S,

$$l_S = \frac{1}{2\sigma^2}\left[\|\bar{y}\|^2 - \langle\bar{y},\bar{u}\rangle^2\right] \tag{C.8}$$

that needs to be minimized over $\bar{\theta}'$.

C.2 SPLINE-BASED SMOOTHING

In this example, the regression model depends linearly on the parameters $\overline{\alpha} = (\alpha_0, \alpha_1, \ldots, \alpha_{M-1})$ defined in Eq. 1.10. Denoting $B_{j,4}(x_i; \overline{b})$ by $B_{j,4}[i]$ and $(B_{j,4}[0], B_{j,4}[1], \ldots, B_{j,4}[N-1])$ by $\overline{B}_{j,4}$, we can express L_S (c.f., Eq. 1.11) in the compact form

$$L_S \quad = \quad \frac{1}{2\sigma^2} \|\overline{y} - \overline{\alpha}\mathbf{B}\|^2 \,, \tag{C.9}$$

$$= \quad \frac{1}{2\sigma^2} \left[\|\overline{y}\|^2 - 2\overline{y}\mathbf{B}^T\overline{\alpha}^T + \overline{\alpha}\mathbf{B}\mathbf{B}^T\overline{\alpha}^T \right] \,, \tag{C.10}$$

$$B_{ji} \quad = \quad B_{j,4}[i] \,. \tag{C.11}$$

Let $\widehat{\alpha}$ be the minimizer of L_S over $\overline{\alpha}$ keeping the other parameters fixed. Using the standard condition for the extremum,

$$\left. \frac{\partial L_s}{\partial \alpha_i} \right|_{\widehat{\alpha}} = 0 \quad \Rightarrow \quad \widehat{\alpha} = \overline{y}\mathbf{B}^T(\mathbf{B}\mathbf{B}^T)^{-1} \,. \tag{C.12}$$

Substituting $\widehat{\alpha}$ into Eq. C.10 gives the fitness function l_S,

$$l_S \quad = \quad \frac{1}{2\sigma^2} \left[\|\overline{y}\|^2 - \overline{y}\mathbf{B}^T(\mathbf{B}\mathbf{B}^T)^{-1}\mathbf{B}\overline{y}^T \right] \,. \tag{C.13}$$

that is to be minimized over the remaining parameters.

Bibliography

[1] T.W. Anderson. *An introduction to multivariate statistical analysis*. Wiley Series in Probability and Statistics. Wiley, 2003.

[2] Mauro Birattari and Marco Dorigo. How to assess and report the performance of a stochastic algorithm on a benchmark problem: mean or best result on a number of runs? *Optimization letters*, 1(3):309–311, 2007.

[3] Sergio Boixo, Troels F Rønnow, Sergei V Isakov, Zhihui Wang, David Wecker, Daniel A Lidar, John M Martinis, and Matthias Troyer. Evidence for quantum annealing with more than one hundred qubits. *Nature Physics*, 10(3):218, 2014.

[4] Daniel Bratton and James Kennedy. Defining a standard for particle swarm optimization. In *Swarm Intelligence Symposium, 2007. SIS 2007. IEEE*, pages 120–127. IEEE, 2007.

[5] Jie Chen, Bin Xin, Zhihong Peng, Lihua Dou, and Juan Zhang. Optimal contraction theorem for exploration–exploitation tradeoff in search and optimization. *IEEE Transactions on Systems, Man, and Cybernetics-Part A: Systems and Humans*, 39(3):680–691, 2009.

[6] Gerda Claeskens and Nils Lid Hjort. *Model selection and model averaging*, volume 330. Cambridge University Press, 2008.

[7] Maurice Clerc. *Particle swarm optimization*, volume 93. John Wiley & Sons, 2010.

[8] Maurice Clerc and James Kennedy. The particle swarm-explosion, stability, and convergence in a multidimensional complex space. *Evolutionary Computation, IEEE Transactions on*, 6(1):58–73, 2002.

[9] Carl de Boor. On calculating with b-splines. *Journal of Approximation Theory*, 6(1):50 – 62, 1972.

[10] Carl de Boor. *A practical guide to splines*, volume 27 of *Applied mathematical sciences*. Springer, 2001.

[11] R. C. Eberhart and Y. Shi. Comparing inertia weights and constriction factors in particle swarm optimization. In *Proceedings of the 2000 Congress on Evolutionary Computation*, volume 1, pages 84–88. IEEE, 2000.

[12] Russell C Eberhart, Yuhui Shi, and James Kennedy. *Swarm intelligence*. Elsevier, 2001.

[13] Bradley Efron. Bootstrap methods: another look at the jackknife. In *Breakthroughs in statistics*, pages 569–593. Springer, 1992.

[14] Andries P Engelbrecht. *Fundamentals of computational swarm intelligence*, volume 1. Wiley Chichester, 2005.

[15] Jerome Friedman, Trevor Hastie, and Robert Tibshirani. *The elements of statistical learning*, volume 1 of *Springer series in statistics*. Springer, 2001.

[16] Jerome H. Friedman. Multivariate adaptive regression splines. *The Annals of Statistics*, 19(1):1–67, 03 1991.

[17] Akemi Gálvez and Andrés Iglesias. Efficient particle swarm optimization approach for data fitting with free knot b-splines. *Computer-Aided Design*, 43(12):1683–1692, 2011.

[18] Andrew Gelman, John B Carlin, Hal S Stern, and Donald B Rubin. *Bayesian data analysis*. Chapman and Hall/CRC, 1995.

[19] Ian Goodfellow, Yoshua Bengio, and Aaron Courville. *Deep learning.* The MIT press, 2016.

[20] W. Hardle. *Applied Nonparametric Regression*, volume 19 of *Econometric Society Monographs.* Cambridge University Press, 1990.

[21] C. W. Helstrom. *Statistical Theory of Signal Detection.* Pergamon, 1968.

[22] Mark W Johnson, Mohammad HS Amin, Suzanne Gildert, Trevor Lanting, Firas Hamze, Neil Dickson, R Harris, Andrew J Berkley, Jan Johansson, Paul Bunyk, et al. Quantum annealing with manufactured spins. *Nature*, 473(7346):194, 2011.

[23] N.L. Johnson, S. Kotz, and N. Balakrishnan. *Continuous univariate distributions*, volume 2 of *Wiley series in probability and mathematical statistics: Applied probability and statistics.* Wiley & Sons, 1995.

[24] David LB Jupp. Approximation to data by splines with free knots. *SIAM Journal on Numerical Analysis*, 15(2):328–343, 1978.

[25] S. Kay. *Fundamentals of Statistical Signal Processing, Volume II: Detection Theory.* Prentice Hall, 1998.

[26] Steven Kay. *Fundamentals of Statistical Signal Processing, Volume I: Estimation Theory.* Prentice Hall, 1993.

[27] J. Kennedy and R. C. Eberhart. Particle swarm optimization. In *Proceedings of the IEEE International Conference on Neural Networks: Perth, WA, Australia*, volume 4, page 1942. IEEE, 1995.

[28] Scott Kirkpatrick, C Daniel Gelatt, and Mario P Vecchi. Optimization by simulated annealing. *Science*, 220(4598):671–680, 1983.

[29] Donald E Knuth. *The art of computer programming, 2: seminumerical algorithms.* Addison Wesley, 1998.

[30] S. Kotz, N. Balakrishnan, and N.L. Johnson. *Continuous multivariate distributions, volume 1: Models and applications.* Wiley series in probability and statistics. Wiley, 2004.

[31] Erich L Lehmann and Joseph P Romano. *Testing statistical hypotheses.* Springer Texts in Statistics. Springer, 2006.

[32] Calvin Leung. Estimation of unmodeled gravitational wave transients with spline regression and particle swarm optimization. *SIAM Undergraduate Research Online (SIURO)*, 8, 2015.

[33] Soumya D Mohanty. Spline based search method for unmodeled transient gravitational wave chirps. *Physical Review D*, 96(10):102008, 2017.

[34] Jorge Nocedal and Stephen J Wright. *Numerical optimization.* Springer Series in Operations Research and Financial Engineering. Springer, 2006.

[35] Marc E Normandin, Soumya D Mohanty, and Thilina S Weerathunga. Particle swarm optimization based search for gravitational waves from compact binary coalescences: performance improvements. *Physical Review D*, 98:044029, 2018.

[36] Yiannis G Petalas, Konstantinos E Parsopoulos, and Michael N Vrahatis. Memetic particle swarm optimization. *Annals of Operations Research*, 156(1):99–127, 2007.

[37] C.R. Rao. *Linear statistical inference and its applications.* Wiley Series in Probability and Statistics. Wiley, 2009.

[38] Christian Robert and George Casella. *Monte Carlo statistical methods.* Springer Texts in Statistics. Springer, 2005.

[39] Jacob Robinson and Yahya Rahmat-Samii. Particle swarm optimization in electromagnetics. *IEEE Transactions on Antennas and Propagation*, 52(2):397–407, 2004.

[40] Jeffrey S Rosenthal. *A first look at rigorous probability theory*. World Scientific Publishing Company, 2006.

[41] Sheldon M Ross. *Stochastic processes*. Wiley, New York, second edition, 1996.

[42] David Ruppert, Matthew P Wand, and Raymond J Carroll. *Semiparametric regression*, volume 12. Cambridge University Press, 2003.

[43] Yuhui Shi and Russell Eberhart. A modified particle swarm optimizer. In *The 1998 IEEE International Conference on Evolutionary Computation*, pages 69–73. IEEE, 1998.

[44] Francisco J Solis and Roger J-B Wets. Minimization by random search techniques. *Mathematics of Operations Research*, 6(1):19–30, 1981.

[45] Rainer Storn and Kenneth Price. Differential evolution– a simple and efficient heuristic for global optimization over continuous spaces. *Journal of Global Optimization*, 11(4):341–359, 1997.

[46] Rangarajan K Sundaram. *A first course in optimization theory*. Cambridge University Press, 1996.

[47] Grace Wahba. *Spline models for observational data*. SIAM, 1990.

[48] Y. Wang and S.D. Mohanty. Particle swarm optimization and gravitational wave data analysis: Performance on a binary inspiral testbed. *Physical Review D*, 81:063002, 2010.

[49] Wikipedia contributors. Errors-in-variables models — Wikipedia, the free encyclopedia, 2018. [Online; accessed 15-July-2018].

[50] Wikipedia contributors. Hertzsprung-Russell diagram — Wikipedia, the free encyclopedia, 2018. [Online; accessed 25-July-2018].

[51] Wikipedia contributors. Pearson correlation coefficient — Wikipedia, the free encyclopedia, 2018. [Online; accessed 10-August-2018].

[52] David H Wolpert and William G Macready. No free lunch theorems for optimization. *IEEE Transactions on Evolutionary Computation*, 1(1):67–82, 1997.

[53] Mauricio Zambrano-Bigiarini, Maurice Clerc, and Rodrigo Rojas. Standard particle swarm optimisation 2011 at CEC-2013: A baseline for future PSO improvements. In *2013 IEEE Congress on Evolutionary Computation (CEC)*, pages 2337–2344. IEEE, 2013.

Index